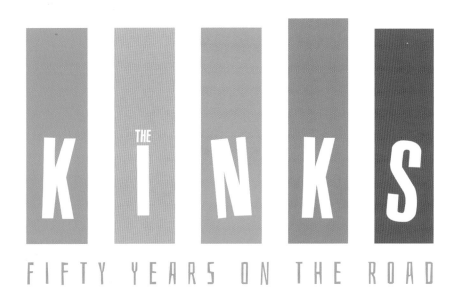

THE KINKS

FIFTY YEARS ON THE ROAD

First Published by FHE Ltd

CAT NO: BZB0331

Photography courtesy Pictorial Press, Wikimedia Commons, Getty Images unless indicated otherwise.

ISBN: 978-1-912332-05-2

Contents

THE KINKS

CHAPTER 1 – THE KINKS IN REVIEW

If there is one band that soundtracks the sixties perfectly its The Kinks. In a series of brilliant singles and albums, they eloquently detailed the legendary decade. They then went on to break America in the seventies before finally retiring in the mid-nineties.The sixties were dominated by the Beatles, but if there was one songwriter who could easily match the sheer imagination and songwriting skill of the Fab Four it was Ray Davies of the Kinks.

Ray was the chief songwriter in the band and the core of the group along with his brother Dave. The pair of them were at each others' throats for a good chunk of the band's career – a creative tension that was key to the band's soul. It was a tension that would spill out in fights between band members, and one that prevented them from becoming the biggest British band apart from the Beatles.

The classic Kinks lineup saw the songwriting genius of Ray Davies excel, weaving in seamlessly with his younger brother's fantastic guitar playing, and the powerful and innovative rhythm section of bass player Peter Quaife and drummer Mick Avory.The Kinks had a bumpy ride, bouncing from electric success to disappointing flops. They made bad mistakes and were bloody-minded in their approach.

They also wrote brilliant songs, from the initial flurry of pure rock excitement to their late-sixties output, when Davies's songwriting really flourished with brilliant lyrics and music that defined Englishness in a way that has become truly influential in the following decades.

They debuted with 'You Really Got Me', one of the most exciting and adrenalised singles in the history of British rock 'n' roll. Their initial sound was cranked excitement. There was a danger about them, a whiff of cordite excitement. They were punk, 13 years before punk, and with the distorted riffing of 'You Really Got Me', they arguably invented the cranked heavy metal riff years before anyone else got there. The band peppered the sixties charts with idiosyncratic, witty songs that virtually single-handedly invented the whole notion of Englishness in pop music. Their influence has been enormous.

Any band that writes clever words with a touch of social realism and has a wry take on the world gets compared to The Kinks. Their shadow hung over the punk scene, with the Jam in particular taking the Davies blueprint of angular social comment, whilst the Pretenders covered 'Stop Your Sobbing', with Chrissie Hynde even having a fling with the head Kink. The Stranglers hit the top 10 with a cover of 'All Of The Day And All Of The Night'. Their fingerprints were all over punk, from the electric shock riffling of their early sound to the social commentary which pervaded the whole scene.

Their influence reverberates through each pop generation. Blur and Oasis owe them a debt and arguably every band in the mid-nineties explosion of British bands was touched by The Kinks, an influence that has carried on with such modern bands as the Kaiser Chiefs and the Arctic Monkeys.

Not only was Ray Davies the first, he was also arguably the best, his classic songs sounding like play-for-today vignettes from a long-lost Britain. With a witty slant he gently pulled apart the class system, singing about England in a run of albums that for a decade were pop perfection.

The Kinks spent the late sixties and early seventies creating classic concept albums that sang of lost Englishness, alcoholism, the trials and tribulations of the music industry and emigrating to Australia. They sang about the older generation and of being misfits.

Ray Davies never followed fashion, whilst London was swinging and rock stars thought they were untouchable, Davies sang of real lives and real people with a keen observational eye, all the time with a personal slant. One of the big four British bands of the sixties along with the Rolling Stones, the Beatles, and the Who. The Kinks never had quite the commercial success of their peers, but their influence has been as big. Pete Townsend always cited them as one of his favourite bands and once stated that Ray Davies should be made Poet Laureate.

He's right.
This is the story of The Kinks.

CHAPTER 2 – THE EARLY YEARS

Ray Davies was born in June 1944 in Muswell Hill. Sitting on top of a hill near Alexandra Palace, Muswell Hill was a staid, respectable neighbourhood.

The Davies were a large working-class family who had moved after the Second World War from inner London to the Muswell Hill/Highgate end of town, literally going up in the world. Ray and Dave were the seventh and eighth arrivals in a big family with an age spread of 25 years. They had six elder sisters and grew up in a female-dominated environment.

Despite being the only boys in a large family dominated by women, the Davies bothers were not particularly close. The three-year gap between them was probably too great to bridge. Three years is an awful lot for young boys, and it can seem like a generation apart.

The brothers grew up in an open house with a large number of relatives passing through. Dave Davies has recalled that instead of having a TV, they would make their own entertainment. On Saturday nights, everyone would go over to the Davies house and there would be a big singsong around the piano. Their mother would sing after a few drinks and their father would dance. This was a gregarious and happy household. It sounds like another world.

Music was an integral part of the boys' background when they were growing up. Ray Davies has remembered his father imbuing him with a love of music with his tap dancing and listening to Jack Buchan, Fred Astaire, Gene Kelly, and Max Miller.

His elder sisters were in love with the pop music of the fifties, the older ones playing Frank Sinatra and the younger ones the Teddy Bears, Perry Como, and the Crew Cuts. Some of the Davies sisters played piano, and Davies senior played the banjo.

Music was everywhere, almost seeping out of the household's walls. It was the perfect background and one that naturally bent the ears of the youngest siblings. With their shared love of music the Davies brothers started to grow closer to each other. They had something in common at last.

Ray got his first guitar when he was 13. His sister Rene showed him a few chords. She died soon after from a heart attack after a night out. Ray continued to play the guitar, learning more chords from one of his brothers-in-law. He had been bitten by the bug, like many teenagers in the late-fifties UK, fired by rock 'n' roll and the glamour of playing guitar. It seemed impossibly exciting and glamorous in staid old fifties Britain.

Dave got his first guitar a year later, when he was 11. Before that he was constantly picking up Ray's guitar. Both brothers would go round to their brother-in-law's flat, where they would swap chords and listen to records, even recording demo's on his tape recorder, which was the first tape recorder any of them had ever seen and a rare item to own in the austere fifties.

The first musician to really blow their minds was Big Bill Broonzy. Turned onto the errant Broonzy by their uncle, they were hooked. Broonzy was a prolific artist who recorded over 350 blues songs. Born at the tail end of the nineteenth century in the Mississippi Delta, in 1924 he moved to Chicago, where he learned guitar and banjo before recording his own folk blues records. In the fifties he toured extensively across Europe.

Broonzy was one of the pioneers of the Chicago blues style and very much a cult figure in the blues revival of the sixties, which he missed, having died of throat cancer in 1958.

Relatively ignored in their homeland, blues artists were cult figures in the UK. Most of the sixties generation were learning their chops by playing along with the great crackling records that passed from hand to hand like valuable items. Dave Davies was just another skinny young guitarist trying to cop the great bluesman's licks. It was a great education for the young guitar player.

Eventually the young Davies brothers were confident enough to get onstage and play. They got the occasional gig at a pub in Clissold Park, where the 12-year-old Dave had to be sneaked in. Here they played their instrumentals for the local drinkers. The pair of them attended a local secondary school, which they both detested. The younger Davies would skive off, bunking around to a mate's house where he smoked and listened to blues records, whilst his older brother bucked the school system, hating the lack of individuality it tried to enforce.

At school, Ray met Pete Quaife, who was in his year. Quaife was born on the 31st of December 1943 in Tavistock, Devon, and started to play with the brothers, playing guitar when they went over to his house and jammed.

> " I heard that Ray and Dave formed the band. That's bullocks! It was Ray and I who formed the band. "
>
> Pete Quaife

They soon added Quaife's friend John Stuart on drums. They started playing concerts at their school as The Ray Davies Quartet. Soon, they were playing background instrumentals at beauty contests as the girls paraded up and down. At gigs other than beauty contests they played Buddy Holly covers and guitar instrumentals, till another school friend turned them on to Chuck Berry.

Berry's hard-rocking songs with clever and witty lyrics had made a firm impression on the UK's aspiring young bands. His song lyrics' sexual tension and humour, combined with the brazen excitement of his rhythmically exciting music cranked loud, was perfect for the rowdy nature of the up-and-coming groups.

In 1962 Dave got expelled from school after getting caught on Hampstead Heath with a girl. It was a buzz for the young tearaway, but the outlaw thrill was swiftly dashed when his mother sent him out to look for work, resulting in the drudgery of interchangeable jobs. His elder brother was at a loose end as well, about to leave school. His art teacher, noted that the gangly youth liked music and running. It was also in 1962 that the band picked up their own management in the shape of Robert Wace and Grenville Collins. A more unlikely pair of showbiz hustlers would be hard to find. Collins worked in the London Stock Exchange, whilst Wace had been to Marlborough College. Bored with their current occupations, the pair started hanging around Denmark Street.

The street, also known as Tin Pan Alley, was the nerve centre of the British music scene, with its guitar shops and cafes and small publishing houses – a real hive of activity. Wace was keen to make it as a singer on his own and was looking for a band to back him up. Looking for suitable musicians from contacts in Denmark Street, they got the tip off about the young band up in Muswell Hill. They went up and checked out the Davies brothers and came to an arrangement that the young band would back up Wace.

They played a real ad hoc selection of gigs backing him up, from tough East End boozers to posh parties in Chelsea. It was a real eye-opener for the 16-year-old Dave, who later remembered that the first time he ever drank champagne was whilst watching the toffs dance stiffly to the band's bump-and-grind R&B at one Chelsea party. Already, the younger Davies brother was the wild man of the group, dressing crazily in thigh-length boots and even taking to carrying a sword around for show.

Sensing that they could really make a go of this, the band politely asked Wace and Collins if they would prefer to be just their managers and let Ray be the singer of the group.

It was so blindingly obvious that this was the way to go that the upper-crust pair took the opportunity to assume the roles in life that they were made for and the classic Kinks line-up was born. The band clicked and the gigs increased. They even got shows outside London, playing the fertile club scene in Manchester. It was in Manchester that they felt there was something beginning to happen, as they started to get real fans there – a real following.

Their managers' upper-crust background was a gift to Ray Davies. He used his experience of some of the early gigs they'd played at the Chelsea parties as background for some of his greatest lyrics. These experiences would end up appearing in some of his sharper lyrical observations on the British class system that became a real staple of his classic songwriting period.

In September 1962, Ray went to Hornsey Art College. There were few bands of that generation that were not touched by the art-school environment. Art school was the classic breeding ground of sixties rock 'n' rollers. From the Beatles to the Stones, most of the bands had some kind of art school background. It was the perfect place to get immersed in culture and to get hip, and it infused the sixties British pop scene with an artsy flavour that made it so different from the scene across the Atlantic.

At first, the predominant music in the art schools had been trad jazz, with earnest students in duffel coats digging the jazz scene. When Lonnie Donegan hit the charts with his cover of Leadbelly's 'Rock Island Line' things changed. Music had become really accessible, and anyone could participate. The beauty of skiffle was its simplicity. The Glasgow-born Donegan started a musical revolution. His pared-down folk and rock 'n' roll was relatively simple to copy, and during the skiffle boom, anyone who wanted to be in a band could suddenly give it a go. If the Davies brothers never directly played skiffle, the idea that a person could just get up and play affected them as it did thousands of teenagers up and down the country.

The skiffle boom gave way to the blues revival, and the names that were being dropped were John Lee Hooker, Muddy Waters and Otis Spann.

A new generation of bands was mixing the electric blues and rock 'n' roll, adding rhythm to the blues, with a dash of Chuck Berry, creating rhythm and blues and fusing it into a culture of their own. On the London circuit the Rolling Stones were playing the handful of small clubs open to this new style in the city. This was the musical backdrop to Ray Davies' art school years.

At art school, Davies studied to be a theatre director, but it was a gig by British blues mentor Alexis Korner at the college late in 1962 that had a much greater bearing on his life. After the gig he went up and met Korner, who was the key figure in the British blues underground.

He'd had a big hand in bringing the Stones together and had connected many other aspiring young blues musicians on the scene. Korner suggested that the young Davies should go and meet Giorgio Gomelsky, who was then the Rolling Stones' manager, and Gomelsky gave him a gig sitting in with an ad hoc band at his club. It was an in.

In 1963 Ray joined the Dave Hunt Band as a guitar player. That night Davies also saw the Rolling Stones play and realised just what kind of band he could and should be in. He was particularly taken by just how cool Brian Jones looked, and was turned on by the band's ragged excitement.

That summer, 1963, the Beatles broke through big and turned the British music scene upside down. From being a pop backwater greeting American pop with open arms, the UK was suddenly engulfed in an enormous rush of energy, a veritable youthquake. All up and the down the country young bands who had formed in the late-fifties' skiffle boom and had moved on to playing beat music were being checked out by the previously uninterested music business.

The Beatles being from Liverpool changed everything. Suddenly, being a regional band was cool. No longer did music executives ignore groups like the Animals in Newcastle or Them in Belfast or treat them like country bumpkins. It seemed as if great bands were pouring out of the woodwork everywhere.

11

While Ray was hanging out with his art-school buddies in the West End and occasionally still jamming with his brother, Dave had kept some kind of band going in Muswell Hill with Pete Quaife, christening them The Ravens after a Vincent Price film.

They played the odd gig, but nothing much was happening. Ray, meanwhile, in late 1963, drifted to the theatre department of Croydon College for a few months before deciding to join his brother's band and make a go of it.

The two brothers were at their closest. Whilst Dave had the sharp street suss, Ray had the drive and determination to break out. They rehearsed hard and started playing on the gig circuit.

The band were well-placed, being smack in the middle of London, right under the nose of the music business.

The only problem was that even with their management team they had no real in to the music industry. Despite the Beatles' mega success, the business was still run by a tiny little clique from Denmark Street looking after its own interests. The Ravens' managers needed a contact to get into the inner circle and they needed it fast.

In late 1963, the band hooked up with Larry Page, a fifties pop star tuned showbiz hustler, who was instantly struck by how green the boys were. He had seen them hanging around Denmark Street, clearly unsure of what to do. Page, though, was instantly struck by the band and told them that Ray Davies was doing a good enough job of the singing despite the Ravens only playing covers. Nonetheless, Page agreed to help and agreed to act as their publisher.

"It used to blow hot and cold with the Kinks on the road. It could be absolutely euphoric or a real downer."

Mick Avory

In November 1963 the band recorded a demo at Regent Sound which included such songs as Slim Harpo's 'Got Love If You Want It' and the Coasters' 'I'm A Hog For You Baby'. They even managed to sneak in one of Ray's first compositions 'It's Alright', as well as two songs written by Dave: 'One Fine Day' and 'I Believed You'. The demo was rough and ready, full of a sprightly energy, if lacking in originality. The band had crossed their style with some Merseybeat inflections, perhaps hoping to catch the current wave that was sweeping over the music scene.Hawking the tapes around, the management team saw little success, with two out of the big four labels, Phillips and Decca, turning the band down straight away. Page, though, managed to get a singer from Coventry called Shel Naylor to cover 'One Fine Day'.

It was that version of the song with a young Jimmy Page playing session guitar on it, which came to be picked up by American producer Shel Tamy. Tamy is a key player in the story of the early Kinks. Born in Chicago in 1937, he moved to London in 1962 on a short trip looking for work. He basically bagged himself production work with record labels after making up a CV. It paid off; he produced a top-10 hit for the Bachelors and suddenly became a Golden boy at Pye records, where he was actively looking for other bands with which to work. He liked the Shel Naylor cover and asked to hear more. Wace had a meeting with him and played him the rough-and-ready five-song acetate.

Tamy was astute enough to pick up on the songs on the demo. He knew there was something there. He signed the band to Pye records, and after only a few months the group was ready to go. Once signed, they decided that it was time to get themselves a better name and chose the apt moniker of The Kinks.

The early sixties were kinky times. The word was all over London that winter, with The Avengers on TV creating excitement over Honor Blackman's supposedly kinky outfits. Also, with the Profumo scandal breaking out all over the newspapers, the sexual peccadilloes of the ruling classes were being laid bare for everybody to see.
The upper classes were rapidly coming to be seen as hypocritical rather than stuffy. Britain was now kinky, not austere as it had been in the fifties.

The germination of the name is something about which several different parties disagree. Wace has claimed that the group members were horrified by it at first when he suggested it. Page has claimed that he came up with it, as well as arranging for photo sessions of the band wearing kinky boots and leathers. Dave Davies has claimed that he already dressed like that and that the band thought of the name themselves.

At any rate, The Kinks was the perfect name for the band. It gave them an aura of outrage and was a tool for grabbing attention quickly when they needed it. Mock outrage had not done the Rolling Stones any harm as they attempted to emulate the runaway success of the Beatles. The name did indeed cause a mini ripple. It got them mentioned on TV on Ready Steady Go, where there were eyebrows raised over the name of this new band. Such innocent times!

Things were moving fast. They now needed an agent, so Wace hustled them a gig at a hip London showbiz restaurant. Once there, he manoeuvred promoter Arthur Howes, who was dining there, into seeing them. Howes, whose stock was rising swiftly because he had spotted The Beatles and given them their first tour, was blown away with the band. He gave them their first tour in March 1964. This sudden break meant that Pye were going to have to go full steam ahead and have the group get a record out. Because everything was moving so fast it was time for some legal paperwork to be drawn up.

The Kinks' management situation was already relatively complex, with Wace and Collins as one party and Page also having some sort of share. Now they also had Arthur Howes and Shel Tamy taking an interest in the band. It was a complex, combustible situation involving varying vested interests, and a dodgy situation for any young band to find themselves in, a minefield that would one day cause them some problems. However, like any young band they just signed any pieces of paper that were put in front of them.

In January 1964 they signed to Pye records, or rather their management signed them to Pye records, since they were not old enough to sign a contract legally themselves. Pye Records was the poor relation to such bigger labels as EMI. However, one advantage of being a small label was that they could move quickly. Pye had already snuck in and signed the Searchers, who were, perhaps, the second best band to come out of that Liverpool scene after the Beatles, in the middle of the Merseybeat boom, and were riding high on a series of Searchers hits.

By 1964, the label had correctly sussed that Merseybeat was running out of steam, and it was looking further afield for whatever musical action was happening next. The Liverpool groups were already being fast-tracked to conventional showbiz success, and the spotlight was now turning on groups that promoters perceived as being more rough and ready and less likely to stand there grinning in mohair suits – groups like the Rolling Stones, whose surly, lewd R&B was making waves.

Pye records were not sure what to do with their new charges, and The Kinks' first few months on the record label were littered with Pye's attempts to find a way to market their new charges and to counter attempts by Ray Davies to resist this.

That January, a week after they signed, they went straight to the studio to record four songs including 'I Took My Baby Home', 'You Still Want Me',' and a cover of Little Richard's 'Long Tall Sally'. It was the first time the band had been in a proper studio, their initial demo having been a low-budget session. They had never heard themselves properly before and were wide-eyed at the playbacks. Ray has reported still remembering his brother turning to him and saying that he had a really commercial voice.

'Long Tall Sally' and 'I Took My Baby Home' was the first Kinks single, released a week later in February, swiftly followed by 'You Still Want Me' and 'You Do Something To Me' that April.
The green young group can be heard in these tracks, which sound less like The Kinks than they do some bouncing Merseybeat outfit. The only thing that made their first two singles stand out was the power of the rhythm section, pushed high and hard by Shel Tamy's mix. This was something the Merseybeat groups, who were in thrall to the rhythm guitar, lacked. Also in place was Ray's distinctive voice.

Unfortunately, the singles disappeared, drowned out by a huge wave of similar Merseybeat knock-offs in the wake of the Beatles' wild success. 'Long Tall Sally' had already been covered to great effect by the Beatles themselves, and The Kinks' version was one cover too many. The record failed to chart. In addition to getting their debut singles out, they brought in a new drummer, Mick Avory, who had actually played one gig with the Rolling Stones and had a jazz background. Avory had gone to audition for the

Stones at the Bricklayers Arms in Soho, but had decided that he didn't want to go full time and couldn't take the gig. Now kicking himself at this missed opportunity, he was determined to give The Kinks a go. He was relieved when he went to the audition and heard they were playing a similar, hard-edged, Chuck-Berry-influenced style.

The others were keen on Avory because he was the same age and had the same aspirations, so they asked him to join. The classic Kinks lineup was finally in place for a tour that March supporting the Dave Clarke Five.

The flop of the first single failed to derail the band, who managed to grab plenty of press attention with their name and a bunch of photo sessions living up to their, well, kinkiness. This was due to the efforts of their management team of Wace, Collins, and Page, who imaginatively hyped The Kinks to the hilt.

First there was the band looking suitably kinky brandishing whips and wearing long boots in a full-page advert in the NME. Page then got them onto Ready Steady Go, the top pop-music TV show in the country. He rented kids to pretend they were fans and charge at the band outside whilst waving banners with 'The Kinks' felt-tipped on them. It was an attempt to recreate a mini Beatlemania riot. They were then hustled into a whole run of teen magazines as the hip, sharp-dressing, kinky new band on the block.

The band members were distinctly uncomfortable with their thrust-upon image. Their early publicity shots show them reacting to their new look in varying ways, from Ray looking uncomfortable to Dave carrying off each successive look like a sharp little clotheshorse. Dave also had the added gimmick of having the longest hair on the scene, far longer than even the Stones had dared to go.

They then pulled back from the kinky hype and were next presented as sharp mods about town, with a distinctly kinky flavour. This was something with which they seemed more comfortable, apart from Ray, who was far too individualistic to be told what to do by anybody. When Page told him to do something about the gap in his teeth he played out his first mini rebellion. He had the teeth temporarily filled in, but when he went back to get the job finished he backed out, fed up with people messing around with him.

Finally, after the Dave Clarke tour, the band fell upon an image with which they felt comfortable with the arrival of the hunting jackets. This was a look that they would settle on for the first phase of their career.

Despite this, their second single, 'You Still Want Me', was also a flop, not even getting to number 42 like their debut. It totally disappeared. By that May they looked like they were on the fast track to being another casualty on the great pop scrapheap. Pye Records warned them that if they did not have a hit with their next single they were going to be dropped.

THE KINKS ARE HERE TO STAY

The band hit back with 'You Really Got Me', one of the greatest singles of all time. The song was initially a throwaway at the end of a five-track demo that the band had put together at Regent Sound. Ray has remembered that no one seemed to like the song much at the time. When they recorded it that July the first version just did not seem to come out right. It sounded too clean. Ray felt it was too slow and insisted in re-recording it. Pye were stunned and made Wace pay for the recording out of his own pocket, something which still annoys the ex-manager to this day.

The new version justified the messing around. It exploded out of the speakers. When they finally delivered the single to Pye they must have been really excited. When Pye heard it there must have been no doubt that this was going to be the hit. The single exceeded their wildest expectations, gatecrashing the charts on both sides of the Atlantic. The timing was perfect. The Beatles had opened up the world market to British pop, and with the Stones' 'It's All Over Now' riding high, and the Animals' cover of 'House of the Rising Sun' a big hit in the States, there was plenty of space for more bands.

The Kinks' contribution to this explosion of white, urban, British pop was electrifying, an anthem to the very working class aggression that lies at the heart of all great white British music. Music that bypasses the subtle sexual rhythms of the original black music and makes an unsubtle bruising concoction of leering bravado tinged with the neurotic British bashfulness. It was an odd contradiction and one that was played out in many of the British groups of the period but especially by The Kinks.

The song was an instant classic. Hooked around the zigzag riff that was cranked through Dave's Elpico amplifier, it was pure adrenaline. The little green 10-watt Elpico amp had a tinny sound that the brothers hated; they nicknamed it the little green amp.

Dave had been messing around with it. He put its speaker output leads through a Vox AC 30 speaker and then slashed the speaker cone of the Elpico to produce a buzzing, distorted sound. They then re-christened this piece of equipment the fart box.

When put through the bigger AC30 the combination was dynamite. His search for the perfect guitar sound was mind-blowing. It was the dirtiest, nastiest, scuzziest guitar sound ever heard and it powered the single along.

In a stroke the young guitarist had invented heavy metal. His brilliant solo on the song was the first real modern guitar solo and still the greatest guitar solo ever recorded, a blast of teenage adrenaline shot across the bow of a great song.

'You Really Got Me' was a bolt of adrenalised excitement, added to by Tamy's thrilling compression, which squeezed every ounce of excitement out of it. Tamy, again, also made sure the bass and drums were cranked as high as he could, which made the record stand out doubly in a time when rhythm sections were seen but not heard. Mick Avory didn't even get to drum on the single. His studio inexperience meant a session player was drafted in, a familiar early sixties scenario played out by cautious producers. There have also been persistent rumours that another guitar player played some of the rhythm parts on the track, but this was malicious gossip and irrelevant at any rate. The song itself has The Kinks' stamp all over it, and it is still one of the greatest rock songs ever recorded.

> I played it, played it and played it (You Really Got Me) I couldn't stop playing it
>
> Ozzy Osbourne

17

Forty years later the song still sounds thrilling, a real rush of rock 'n' roll adrenalin. At the time it must have sounded like a monster, like the next stage in rock 'n' roll after the Beatles' takeover. On top of this was a vocal like no one had ever heard before. Davies's voice was leering, and yet it had vulnerability and melancholy to it, and all this in a two-minute rush of a frenzied rock 'n' roll song.

The Kinks were suddenly bang smack in the epicentre of early sixties British cool. Loved by the mods for their sharp suits and loved by the frenzied adrenalised youth in the dance halls of the UK because of their fantastic number-one hit that captured the thrilling rush of youth perfectly. By the time the single had sold a million copies they were also number one in America and suddenly right up there with the Beatles as part of the cutting edge of worldwide pop music.

From Zero to hero with the release of one seven-inch single, it was the pop dream come true. The Kinks were suddenly on the conveyer belt. No longer did they have to pay fans to scream for them. No longer did Page have to wheel and deal to get them TV slots. They were now in constant demand and their lives became a never-ending round of interviews and TV appearances. The Kinks had truly arrived.

CHAPTER 3 – THE FIRST ALBUM

You Really Got Me' was a sensation. Within a matter of months The Kinks had hit the pinnacle. They were unlike any of the other groups who had just hit the big time. They were much younger and they were more of a shambles. Their complex management situation was not like the Stones and the Beatles, who both had a firm plan of action. The Kinks, in contrast, were caught on the hop.

With record sales at an all-time high there was no time to waste, and the band was rushed into the studio to record their debut album barely one year after properly forming. The Kinks initial salvos presented them as an adrenaline-filled wild band. It was something that they did not back away from on their relentless tour schedule. They were involved in many road incidents as they lived the rock 'n' roll lifestyle to the hilt. Flushed with success and far younger than their contemporaries – Dave was only 17 at the time – they were full of the adrenalised craziness of a youthful band on the top of their game.

The album was, as expected, full of the swagger and confidence of a young group with their first big break. Half covers and with only six songs from Ray, the album is as patchy as one would expect from a young group in a hurry, one without enough songs to record and falling back on obscure blues covers. Full of boundless energy and excitement, its quality varied from a poor cover of Shel Tamy's 'Bald Headed Woman' to Ray Davies's own classic 'Stop Your Sobbing' (written after Tamy asked for some Beatles-like material.

Then there was 'Just Can't Go To Sleep', where the 20-year-old showed an amazing prowess and sensitivity for someone of his years and presented a real pointer of things to come. It was an early sign of the internal conflict within the band, one brother a songwriter of incredible sensitivity writing songs in a group put together by his younger brother to showcase his incredible musical virtuosity and rawness.

Meanwhile, Dave also led an enthusiastic canter though a cover of Bo Diddley's 'Cadillac' and Don Covay's 'Long Tall Shorty'. The band sound really young on the record and the youthful excitement is put to good use on faster songs like 'Beautiful Delilah', and 'I'm A Lover Not A Fighter".

It has moments of crystalline beauty, such as on the harmonies for 'I Took My Baby Home', but the album reeks generic white-boy-plays-the-blues without the exuberant melodicism of the Beatles or the scowling bad-boy blues sound of the Stones. It's not that it's a bad record, it's just not a great record, apart from 'You Really Got Me'.

As soon as the album was recorded, the band were back on the road, supporting Billie J. Kramer. It was a tour of wild escapades and constantly screaming girls. Like the Beatles, they couldn't hear a note of what they were playing, but just got off on the sheer excitement of the times.

Pop music was at an all–time peak. Never again would it attract as much wild excitement as it did in 1964, when it seemed to be a cathartic release for the whole of the Western world. This was probably due to the Beatles' freakish success.

Pop was reaching places and people it would have never normally have touched. The Kinks were beneficiaries of this, and they were also capable of writing songs as good and as quickly as their Liverpudlian rivals, as the swift germination of their follow-up to 'Really Got Me' proved.

In a call midway though the tour, their publisher asked Ray to write a follow-up to the massive hit. He popped by the office, strummed a few chords, and then arranged the song in a sound check the next day. A couple of days after that they were in the studio and recorded 'All Of The Day And All Of The Night'. When you're at the top of your game everything seems so easy.

Bert Bacharach praised it as a 'neurotic song', and the legendary song writer hit the nail right on the head; it was a youthful, neurotic anthem, a song of possessiveness, as the protagonist wants to be with his girl 'all of the time' in that utterly idealistic, neurotic way of young lovers. Not quite a re-write of their stunning debut, the single takes everything from their first number-one and cranks it a bit further, squeezes it just that little bit tighter.

Recorded in three hours it's the sound of a band full of beans, thrilled by the world and thrilled by their creative powers. Again riding roughshod on another zigzag riff played by Dave, it is an exercise in how to create as much excitement as possible from a two-minute pop song.
It hit the charts as 'You Really Got Me' started its slide down the top 40. It was a chart overlap that saw The Kinks set out on an almost unbroken 14 months of constant presence in the top 40. In 1964, if a band hit the top they were expected to crank out the material.

The work rate of bands during this period was insane. They were either constantly on the road or rushed around TV studios, then, on their days off, expected to record more songs. The record labels were in a blind panic, fearing the bubble could burst at any moment.

As soon as 'All Of The Day And All Of The Night' hit the top three, the boys were ushered back into the studio to record an EP. EPs were very much a sixties staple, as every band would be pimped for four more tracks when they were at the top of their game. The Beatles did them. Everyone did them.

They were neither counted as singles nor as albums – just as something in between. Mid-tour, the band were back in the studio sleepwalking their way through 'Louie Louie', with a tired Ray admitting that he'd sung his vocal whilst reading the Record Mirror.

That December the 20-year-old Ray Davies married a 17-year-old Kinks fan from Bradford named Rasa. Rasa had already inspired 'All Of The Day And All Of The Night', so Ray's feelings for her were publicly documented. Rasa was to be around for the next 10 years and was involved in the family business, even to the extent of singing some of the backing vocals on Kinks singles.

The hectic work rate caused tensions in the band; years later bass player Mick Avory related hating all the fighting all the time. The Kinks were on the treadmill. It was a necessary situation. Pop success is really fleeting and the endless touring, especially in the sixties, was one of the few guarantees of surviving in a vicious, fashion-driven scene.

For the time being, though, the Kinks were one of the hottest bands in the country thanks to two killer singles. They were about to go the States, where they had scored two top-10 hits. The world was at their feet.

The songs on the album were:

BEAUTIFUL DELILAH (Berry)
The first of two Chuck Berry songs opened the album. The track belonged to Dave Davies, who provided a characteristic rasping vocal and frenetic guitar break.

SO MYSTIFYING (RD Davies)
The album's first Ray Davies original showed that he had yet to transcend his influences and find his own voice as a songwriter.

JUST CAN'T GO TO SLEEP (RD Davies)
Ray alluded to the insomnia that plagued him, on this Beatle-like number.

LONG TALL SHORTY (Covay)
The Kinks' version of the mod favourite written by Don Covay and recorded by Pye stablemate Tommy Tucker.

I TOOK MY BABY HOME (RD Davies)
A Merseybeat influence was evident on a song that first appeared as the B-side of Long Tall Sally.

I'M A LOVER NOT A FIGHTER (Miller)
A cover of the JD Miller song originally recorded by first-generation blues singer Lazy Lester, sung by Dave.

YOU REALLY GOT ME (RD Davies)
The Kinks' breakthrough single radiated excitement from the opening distorted guitar riff, a sound created by Dave Davies taking a razor blade to his amp's speaker and almost electrocuting himself in the process. Dissatisfied with the first recorded version, Ray threatened to quit music altogether unless the band was allowed to re-record it. The song is often credited with inventing heavy metal, but Dave preferred to think of it as "the first heavy guitar riff rock record."

CADILLAC (McDaniel)
Bo Diddley (straight name: Ellas McDaniel) was a hero to countless British bands. The Kinks' version of his 'Cadillac' showcased the Chicago guitarist's patented stuttering rhythm.

BALD HEADED WOMAN (Talmy)
Sessionmen Jon Lord on Hammond and Jimmy Page on 12-string guitar were brought in to lend a hand, as the Kinks were unfamiliar with Talmy's song.

REVENGE (RD Davies/Page)

A short, frantic, harmonica-led instrumental jointly credited to Ray Davies and Larry Page.

TOO MUCH MONKEY BUSINESS (Berry)

Chuck Berry's rapid-fire lyric was ill-suited to Ray's voice, but Dave provided a blistering guitar break.

I'VE BEEN DRIVING ON BALD MOUNTAIN (Talmy)

Shel Talmy's second piece sounded rawer than the first due to the absence of the session musicians.

STOP YOUR SOBBING (RD Davies)

Apart from You Really Got Me, this was the album's standout track, and, coincidentally, the only one to feature Mick Avory on drums; elsewhere, he was replaced by session musician Bobby Graham. (The Pretenders' version, their debut single, was a hit in 1979. Ray was to embark on a stormy three-year relationship with head Pretender Chrissie Hynde in 1981.)

GOT LOVE IF YOU WANT IT (Moore)

Ray sang this cover of the Slim Harpo (straight name: James Moore) blues standard in a peculiar nasal whine.

CHAPTER 4 - KINDA KINKS

A month after hitting the top with 'All Of The Day And All Of The Night' The Kinks released their next single, 'Tired Of Waiting For You', the song had originally been recorded for the first album, but Shel Tamy had been astute enough to tell the band to hold it back for a single.The song was an early Ray Davies original, which he had recorded for a demo. When the band recorded the backing track, Ray had not actually finished writing the words. He put the lyrics down virtually off the top of his head at the last minute, minutes after the backing vocals were put down.

They still went back to the studio after that to add some more guitars to the track in order to beef it up a bit, to make it sound more like The Kinks. The original recording was much lighter and needed that trademark sound of zigzag rhythm guitars, which were duly added, although with much less ferocity than on the first two singles.

'Tired of Waiting For You' was a big leap forward for Ray. A deceptively simple song, it showed a sensitivity and songwriting skill that belied his youth. It was also the last of the early Kinks hard-rock singles. Even without the cranked-up wildness of their first two singles, 'Tired Of Waiting For You' still packs a punch. The swaggering energy was harnessed in; its power oozed through it, relying on tension and release. It was the first sure sign of a band progressing forward, understanding its innate power. It was the band's second number-one in the UK and their biggest-ever hit in the USA.

'Tired Of Waiting For You' was a typical love song with a twist from Davies. It also captured the frustrations of a generation kicking against the authorities. The classic sixties zeitgeist that songs like 'Tired Of Waiting For You' caught both musically and, unintentionally, lyrically. Songs that were the soundtrack to a restless generation. The Kinks at this point were at the top of the game.

Within a year they had come from nowhere and were running parallel with the Beatles and the Stones. They had moved to a position to run with those groups and become one of the biggest bands in the world. The pressure of success, though, was beginning to tell, especially on Ray. Somehow he held it together, even when they were bundled straight into the studio to record their second album after returning from an Australian tour in February 1965.

It was as if their label and their management believed that they had to be milked while they were hot and had no confidence in the long-term success of the band. In many ways they were right. The sixties were moving at an incredible pace. The Beatles were releasing singles and albums at an unbelievable rate and also moving forward musically, and so were the Stones. The Kinks would have to go back in the studio six months after recording their debut and attempt to make a more representative album.

The year 1965 found the Kinks within months both of making it and of being in danger of becoming yesterday's men in the fast-moving pop market. Their very success, their very sound, had become a dead weight from which they were becoming desperate to escape.

At the same time they were living the rock 'n' roll lifestyle at full tilt, especially Dave. At 18 he was a young kid on the block and had set about on a three-year partying binge, as would any self-respecting young gunslinger at the top of his game. The touring was, as ever, a blur of wild nights, fights, riots, screaming girls, and madness. It was a bizarre spectacle.

The 1965 Kinks had suddenly gone into creative hyperdrive. Ray was writing songs that were moving further and further away from the template the industry expected of the band. He was into his own idea of putting great art onto a seven-inch single and not giving a damn for the commercial consequences. Luckily, he was also intuitively a great commercial pop songwriter who could combine great art with great pop. The new album, Kinda Kinks, showcased a band hinting at depth and also ready with their own songwriting skills, with only two covers this time.

Released in March 1965, The Kinks' second album saw them as very much an adrenalised beat-boom band, but there was also a keen intelligence lurking just below the surface to hint at what was coming. Even then, the 21-year-old Ray was an astute songwriter and his younger brother was perhaps the most exciting guitar player on the scene, revelling in his rudimentary approach to the guitar that belied a wicked technique that saw him peel off the most exquisite and exciting guitar solos ever heard.

The album showed that Ray was coming into his own as a creator of melodies; it just was not quite there yet. A rushed album, Kinda Kinks is a snapshot from an era. It is a good example of mod-era rock with enough standout tracks to hint at what was to come.
The standout cuts include, 'Look For Me Baby', and 'Come On Now', with the female chorus vocals

provided by Rasa. There is the neo-acoustic folk-jazz of 'Nothin' In The World Can Stop Me Worryin' Bout That Girl'. The powerful ballad, 'Something Better Beginning', was another nod to the style of Ray's future writing with its clever melody and a well-developed storyline with a twisted edge, and 'Tired of Waiting For You' was the first single to hint at the more melancholic Kinks.

The flipside to this melancholia was Dave singing a tongue-in-cheek romp through the blues standard 'Naggin' Woman', and a lame cover of Martha and the Vandellas' 'Dancing in the Street'. Again, not a great album, but there were enough tantalising moments and hints of potential that would maintain the Kinks as contenders.

Just before the album was released in March 1965 they released their next single, an unsuccessful Motown pastiche with 'Everybody's Gonna Be

Happy'. Initially, Ray was worried about the single, feeling that it might not be the right one to keep up their run of fantastic hits. His management assured him that it would not be a problem, but the single stalled at number 20. It was a bad blip in the band's rise to the top. It was the end of their brief flirtation with being equal partners to the Beatles and the Stones in the hierarchy of British pop, and resulted in the single's B-side, 'Who'll Be The Next In Line', being released as their next single in America.

A few weeks later the band was back in the studio trying to get their career back on track with a new song, 'Set Me Free'. They entered the studio trying to write an archetypal Kinks single but without really knowing what an archetypal Kinks song was.

The song was initially written by Ray for Cilla Black to cover, but they added power chords to it in the studio in an attempt to get back to their initial sound. Despite Ray not initially liking the song, it is very much a Kinks classic. Even better was the B-side, 'I Need You', which said everything that 'All Of The Day And All Of the Night' was saying, but in a much more direct and forceful manner.

The songs on the album were:

LOOK FOR ME BABY (RD Davies)
Some interesting lyrics, which hinted at Ray's outsider status and the elusiveness of his real nature, enlivened an otherwise routine affair.

GOT MY FEET ON THE GROUND (RD Davies/D Davies)
A rare songwriting collaboration between the Davies brothers. Sung by Dave, this is one of the more energetic tracks.

NOTHING IN THE WORLD CAN STOP ME WORRYING ABOUT THAT GIRL (RD Davies)
An introspective piece with a suitably mournful blues feel to accompany the title.

NAGGIN' WOMAN (West/Anderson)
Dave provided the lead vocal on this blues workout, the album's second cover version.

WONDER WHERE MY BABY IS TONIGHT (RD Davies)
More uncertainty from the pen of Ray, featuring the brothers duetting on lead vocal.

TIRED OF WAITING FOR YOU (RD Davies)
The Kinks' third hit and second chart-topper, Tired of Waiting For You, adapted the formula of You Really Got Me and All Day into a slower, more reflective groove. Recorded at the sessions for the debut album but held over at Shel Talmy's behest, the song fitted the weary, uncertain feel of the album to a tee.

DANCING IN THE STREET (Stevenson/Gaye)
A tribute to Ray's favourite Motown group, Martha and the Vandellas, this undistinguished version of their most famous song can best be described as filler.

DON'T EVER CHANGE (RD Davies)
Sounding instantly familiar, this song's classy melody made the track one of the album's hidden gems.

COME ON NOW (RD Davies)
A song written by Ray while on tour in Scotland for Dave to sing on the B-side of Tired of Waiting.

SO LONG (RD Davies)
The Kinks ventured into folk territory on this charming acoustic ditty. Ray painted himself as a loner and included reference to his North London roots in Muswell town.

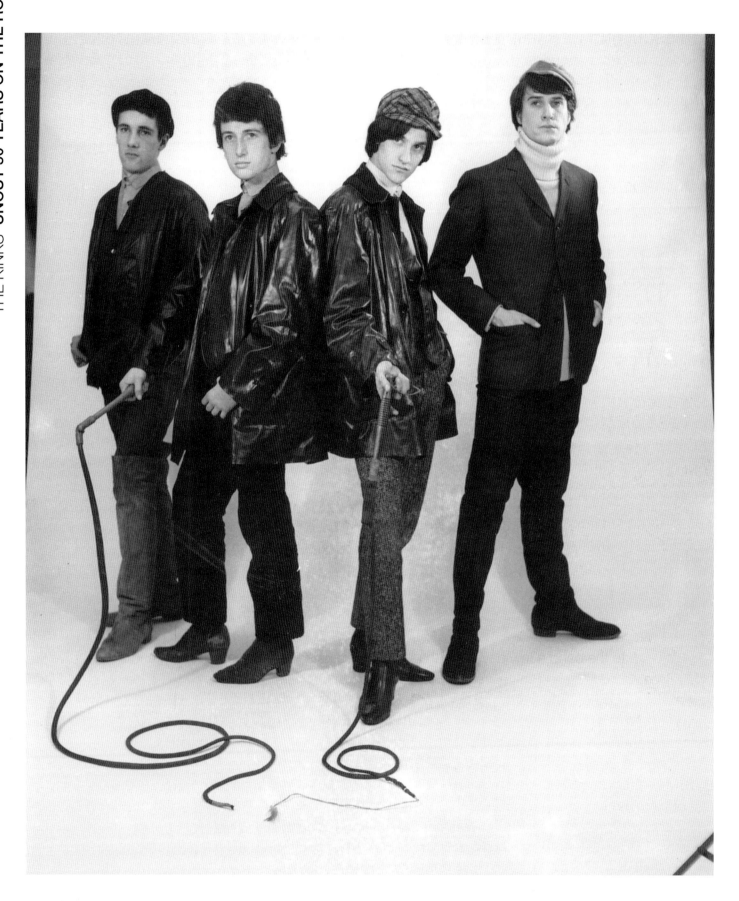

YOU SHOULDN'T BE SAD (RD Davies)

Ray was particularly aggrieved when Shel Talmy informed him that the out-of-sync doubletracking on his lead vocal could not be re-recorded due to a lack of studio time, thus hampering the intended Motown pop-soul feel.

SOMETHING BETTER BEGINNING (RD Davies)

A note of cautious optimism rounded off the album in the shape of this finely honed pop song.

CHAPTER 5 - KINKS KONTROVERSY

With Kinda Kinks in the shops, the band set out on its first headlining tour, and the pressure was now really beginning to tell on them. Ray and Dave were arguing; Dave and Mick Avory had a fight and had to have separate dressing rooms when the group played Cardiff. That night the fight flared up again, but this time it was on stage. During the second song in the set, Dave spat at Mick and the normally stoic drummer got up and hit the hotheaded guitar player with his hi-hat stand, knocking him out. Avory then legged it from the venue with the police in hot pursuit.

At the time it seemed that the band was finished. The tensions were unbearable. The pressure had become too much, and the fight seemed to have driven a wedge between members of the group. Mick retuned to the band a few days later thanks to Larry Page, who insisted that they keep their lineup together for a crack at America. Although Dave and Mick made up, the drummer's quiet nature was a constant source of frustration for him. Dave felt that his ideas were getting pushed to the background by his more dominant older brother and that the rest of the band would not support him in his own creativity, feelings amplified by the hectic touring schedule into which the band were booked.

Page, however, coerced The Kinks into keeping going and sent them straight out on an American tour. They had already scored three top-10 hits in the States and went there as big stars. The American market was far different from the UK's; the bands that were really doing the business over the pond were gimmicky, grinning bands like Herman's Hermits and the Dave Clark Five. Compared to these bands, The Kinks were operating on an entirely different level.

Their appearance on Shindig, the key American pop-music TV show that celebrated the lightweight end of pop, underlined their innate punkiness. Their live show, honed by 18 months of rigorous touring, was just lewd and rude enough to excite Middle America. With his guitar rammed into his crotch, Dave's swaggering was more suggestive than anyone had ever been before on US TV, whilst Ray's brooding persona oozed from the screen. It underlined the difference between the two brothers, a difference that was at the core of the band. The tension between Dave's raw-edged feeling and Ray's brooding intellectuality presented to anyone watching, a radically different kind of performance to Peter Noone's neo-cabaret Hermits. The Kinks were wild.

This was no put-on. The Kinks had become completely out of control. The fractious inter-band relationships, their youthfulness, and the abrasive personalities involved, saw them play out a chaotic, anarchic tour across the States as they firmly pressed the self-destruct button.

At one gig they played 'You Really Got Me' over and over. In between gigs the band's members were not getting on; they travelled at opposite ends of the coach. They would stand at opposite sides of the stage. The atmosphere was electric; it was daggers drawn.

The tour culminated in disaster when the band fell out with a promoter in Sacramento, and there was another incident involving a scuffle with a member of the American Federation Of Musicians, one of several rumoured reasons why The Kinks wound up being banned from playing in America. Another rumour attributed the ban to their refusal to join the union. Mick Avory summed it up eloquently by claiming that the ban was due to a combination of bad management, bad luck, and bad behaviour.

They were banned for four and half years, a total disaster that pretty well totally kiboshed their career in superband terms, America being the key world market. By the time they got back to the States, the sixties were all but over, and pop had moved to a different place. The Kinks could have taken America big time in the sixties and become one of the megagroups of the period, but a combination of their own willfulness and the Americans' curiously stuffy attitudes finished it off for them.

It was just one of many disasters that marred their history. Other, darker theories abounded about why they were banned. One claimed that the Federation became paranoid about the British invasion stealing their market, with the unprecedented success of the Beatles and the Stones meaning that a whole flood of British bands was moving into the American market. The theory was that the AFM might have decided to act to try and stop this takeover, a move that would be illegal as well as unfair, considering just how much the American entertainment industry dominates the world scene.

Mind you, they did not actually ban anyone else, and the Kinks did hit America in 1965 with plenty of bad attitude. The Kinks had played into their hands with an ill-prepared tour which had seen conflicts with American tour promoters after a couple of poorly attended concerts, and a run-in with a union official when they appeared on Dick Clark's TV show.

In many ways, though, they only had themselves to blame. Ray treated headlining a show at the Hollywood Bowl with utter contempt, despite it being a big gig by anyone's standards, and a gig that should have been the pinnacle of two years of hard work, leaving the band on the threshold of breaking the States wide open.

At one point, to the exasperation of his managers, he was refusing to go on stage. It was a combination of Ray attempting to establish his own identity, trying to step away from the machine in the middle of the whirlwind of success, and playing pop-star games. In addition, it was typical of The Kinks' obstinate refusal to play the game, a refusal that in this instance was to shoot them in the foot.

The ban had a dual effect on the band. On the one hand, it cut them off completely from the powerhouse of American culture, meaning they totally missed the flowering of the late-sixties hippie movement and all the external influences that the American scene could have had on them. It meant that, to America, they were very much the outsiders looking in. They were prevented from gaining access to the world's biggest market. They had to sit back and watch as their contemporaries became enormous in America, making the switch from parochial British pop to mainstream rock-stadium success in the States.

The upside of this was that they would become even more quirky and even more quintessentially English, almost as if they were thumbing their noses at American success and underlining their suburban English status. It seemed that The Kinks had decided not to be a big-time rock 'n' roll band. They were not going to go after the kind of success the Beatles and the Stones craved. They were going to wander down a solitary and challenging path of their own.

In 1965 pop began to change. The initial beat boom was dying down, and the energy of the bands was being channelled into a creative flowering. The Beatles had just released Rubber Soul, the first record that flexed their creative muscle and saw them move beyond the mop-top straightjacket.

At the same time The Kinks' 1965 album showed the first stylistic changes in Ray's songwriting style. The album sat between the early Kinks and the about-to-

flower mid-sixties style that would see Davies veering off into the classic songwriting groove, inventing the English style that made his name.

London in 1965 was changing rapidly. The Beatles and the explosion of pop culture had blown apart the stuffy post-war climate. There was a new attitude in town, a swaggering hipness, a smartness, a satirical pop edge. The establishment was being laughed at and to be into pop was to be hip. At the same time, the art school brigade was bending pop into new shapes of hip. The Kinks were pivotal in this, and yet they also sat outside the new hipster elite. It was typical of Ray Davies, perhaps one of the most gifted pop-art commentators of the period, to sit outside what would have been the perfect platform for his instincts.

In the summer of 1965 Davies's songwriting was as sharp and hip as that of the Stones or the Beatles. Songs like 'I Need You' and 'See My Friends' were as ground-breaking and smart as anything that their contemporaries were coming out with, perhaps smarter.Davies was showing a sharp eye for social commentary, arguably the sharpest eye for social commentary around, far keener than the Stones' dark nihilism and the Beatles' own observations.

The problem the Kinks had was that they were not quite mainstream enough to give their commentary validity. The very pop scene that had given them kudos was increasingly becoming less interesting for Ray, who, being the awkward sod that he was, was turning his back on the conventional pop-star game.

The Kinks had become happy to occupy what was then a curious role, that of the outsiders, the misfits. They were about to become the first cult band. If they were not happy with the trappings of pop-star success, they were far more content to be sitting on the sidelines, free to create what they wanted whilst satirising the whole gravy train. It suited them fine.

Instead of licking their wounds after their ignominious hounding out of America, The Kinks released their best single yet, 'See My friends', a single that preceded the craze for all things mystical and Indian by riding in on the sort of raga eastern drone for which the Beatles would get all the credit months later. It was typical of them, being the constant innovators overlooked by the mainstream.

The single was unlike anything that they had done before. This time there was no attempt to ride in roughshod over some variation of that 'You Really Got Me' riff. There was no attempt at beat-group adrenalin. This was a single unlike anything The Kinks or anybody else had ever released before.

It was a harbinger for all that experimentation that was to dominate the swinging sixties and beyond. 'See My Friends' could well have been the first experimental pop single.

On the way back from Australia earlier in the year, the band had stopped off in India, where Ray had sat down on the beach and been intrigued to hear the chanting of local fisherman. India is an amazing country, so rich in cultural intensity that it is a real eye-opener to anyone with a bit of nous. The sights, the smells, and the sounds of the place are fantastically exotic to pale-skinned artists from the cold climes of northern Europe. The music is built on drones. It is incredibly subtle and inspirational. For the resting Davies, lying on the beach and taking a break from the riots and craziness of the never-ending Kinks tours, it must have been an amazing experience just to hear those fishermen singing. That the frontman of a British rock 'n' roll band was being turned on by Indian culture a good year before his contemporaries and actually being there in the flesh, was again typical of the Kinks' innate hipness and cool.

They created the drone on the track by getting Ray's 12-string guitar to feedback in a special way. This was in the days before feedback was a conventional tool in rock 'n' roll recordings. It was again typical of the Kinks and the art school background of their leader that they became interested in twisting sounds, taking what a pop record could be and bending it out of shape and into something else.

It was the perfect marriage of the feel of Indian music translated into the three-minute shock of a Western pop song, and because of this it works on both levels on this song of acceptance. In interviews at the time, Ray talked about the song being about a youth not being sure of his sexuality,

31

about a campness, a closet sexuality that he had experienced in the music industry. Such subtle feelings were not particularly welcome in the big lads' club that was rock 'n' roll.

The drone on the song was so original that it sounded mind-blowing. The Beatles were listening keenly to this new development and picked up on the way the track sounded like a sitar. It fired their imaginations. The Who and Pete Townsend were particularly impressed by their rival's ground-breaking technique, and it influenced Townsend directly on the next Who album.

Hitting his stride, Ray also came up with another Kinks classic, 'A Well Respected Man', which was part of the frightfully titled Kwyet Kinks E.P. The EP showed the band still on the stylistic move. Dave chipped in with a youthful song of self-pity, 'Wait Till The Summer Comes Along', but it was his elder brother's 'A Well Respected Man' that set the stall.

Written whilst on holiday in Torquay where he was sent by the management to take a break from the endless touring, Ray's sharp satirical tongue tore into his newfound respectability by observing the debs at the dances at which the Kinks had once played, and also Grenville's posh background. These were rich pickings for Ray's satirical social eye. The song took a swipe at the rigid social background of the middle classes and juxtaposed them with the sexual desire that was always there just below the surface. It was the first real classic Ray Davies song of social commentary, again a hugely influential approach to songwriting style that others would copy repeatedly in the sixties.

"

When I wrote the song, I had the sea near Bombay in mind. We stayed at a hotel by the sea, and the fishermen come up at five in the morning and they were all chanting. And we went on the beach and we got chased by a mad dog - big as a donkey.

Ray Davies

At this time, The Kinks broke away from Larry Page and his publishing house. It was a situation that they had outgrown. They were already in a minefield of difficult business relationships, and it would take several years of court cases to sort out their business affairs. If there ever was an example of how to mess up the business part of the music biz completely, The Kinks were it. Their swift rise to the top had left them in a legal minefield of conflicting interests, and they had literally come to pay for it.

In November 1965, in the middle of all this, they finally released their ninth single, 'Till the End Of The Day'. The song had been held up by the publishing wrangles. It was another ode to being free and being in control of the situation, another great Davies song about being sexually possessive. It also saw a return to the more strident sound of the earlier singles. It also saw another great Kinks B-side. One great thing about the Kinks was the overall high standard of their work. Not only were the A-sides of their singles gems, like all the best pop bands they had the unerring knack of releasing killer B-sides.

The flipside of 'Till the End Of the Day' was its equal, if not even better. 'Where Have All The Good Times Gone' was a song about the downside of getting to the top. It saw the world weary Ray turn his sharp cynical eye onto the pop industry and being distinctly unimpressed by what he found. The hipster notions of hating your parents and the triumphant bellowings of youth were not of much interest to the traditionalist and individualistic side of Ray's character. This song pointed out that your parents may just have something to offer, some insights that might be worth listening to. This was a revolutionary idea in the context of sixties youth rebellion.

The Kinks released their new album on the back of the single in November 1965. Kinks Kontroversy was the last of their albums to be lumbered with the clumsy use of Ks in the titles. Still, it was aptly titled, as The Kinks were involved in more than a few scrapes during the previous year, with riots at European concerts, a trail of incidents at British gigs and that ban in America. They were never far from controversy, no matter how they spelled it.

Kinks Kontroversy was in an almost subdued style, moving further away from the aggressive shots of their first singles with songs of powerlessness, being lost in the machine and being in a position where a person just can't win – serious subjects covered with the Davies wit. It balanced neatly between the band's old style with the blues riffing of 'Milk Cow Blues', and the zig-zag riff stylings of their early singles on 'Till The End Of The Day'.

There were also hints of Ray's future direction on 'The World Keeps Going Round' and 'I'm On An Island'. Kinks Kontroversy is the first sign of them beginning to wander down their path and Ray Davies's idiosyncratic twist, willful eccentricity, and genius songwriting ability, first flowers here.

The songs on the album were:

MILK COW BLUES (Estes)
The Sleepy John Estes song started the album with its only cover version and a hint of menace in the nagging guitar hook. Dave and Ray alternated on lead vocals.

RING THE BELLS (RD Davies)
Ray was developing into one of the 1960s' greatest pop craftsmen, and Ring the Bells highlighted his growing ability to create a distinct mood for each song.

GOTTA GET THE FIRST PLANE HOME (RD Davies)
Ray's disillusionment with the long foreign tours that preceded the making of the album informed what is otherwise a pedestrian, riff-driven beat song.

WHEN I SEE THAT GIRL OF MINE (RD Davies)
The Kinks' love of girl groups was evident in the melody of this underrated piece, which recalled the Angels', My Boyfriend's Back.

I AM FREE (D Davies)
Dave's first solo songwriting credit betrayed a Bob Dylan influence. His compositions often showed a more reflective side that was at odds with his image as a raver.

TILL THE END OF THE DAY (RD Davies)
The last of The Kinks' great riff-dominated singles and perhaps something of a backward step following the experimentation of See My Friend – but the energy and the harmonies combined in an irresistible package.

THE WORLD KEEPS GOING ROUND (RD Davies)
An intriguing mix of observations – similar to those of John Lennon's on Rain – and Ronettes-style pop.

I'M ON AN ISLAND (RD Davies)
A wry sense of humour was evident on this calypso-tinged ode to isolation.

WHERE HAVE ALL THE GOOD TIMES GONE (RD Davies)
The B-side of Till the End of the Day is another Kinks song made famous by a cover; in this case, David Bowie's version on his 1973 album, Pin-Ups. Ray's obsession with an idealised past reared its head for the first time. Although usually interpreted as deliberately flying in the face of Swinging-Sixties optimism, it was, in reality, a personal reflection.

IT'S TOO LATE (RD Davies)
The Kinks strayed into Rolling Stones territory with chugging guitar and an uncharacteristic note of nastiness in the lyric.

WHAT'S IN STORE FOR ME? (RD Davies)
The answer: a hint of a ska, Shel Talmy on guitar, Ray in the producer's chair, and a fraternal vocal duet.

YOU CAN'T WIN (RD Davies)
More Ray Davies pessimism closed proceedings in similar but in rather less memorable fashion to Where Have All the Good Times Gone.

CHAPTER 6 - FACE TO FACE
The Kinks entered 1966 in the curious position of being commentators on the pop parade that was hustling out of control all around them. The ever-sensitive and troubled Ray Davies' sharp satirical pen was in hyperdrive, and the band's next single was an absolute classic of the form.

'Dedicated Follower Of Fashion' completely summed up everything about London in 1966, tearing into the city's hipster chic in the months before the swinging sixties really erupted. It focuses a journalistic eye on the vacuous world of the scenester moving from one London boutique to another, from one London party to another, slipping in and out of the trends.

The song brilliantly satirises the emptiness of the pop culture that had promised so much but had ended up being just another excuse to dress up and run around in circles. That it came from someone who was perceived as being a central part of that process, someone who was in a band that made its name on sharp dressing and being hip, made the song even better.

Released in February 1966, 'Dedicated Follower Of Fashion' saw the first flowerings of the wry social commentary upon which Ray Davies would make his name, of the astute and wry anthems that summed up the attitude of swinging London and the less fashionable suburban life, from the keen eye of someone sitting on the outside of the scene. Whilst everyone else was desperately underlining their working-class creds, by speaking in cod cockney, for example (in the case of that nice middle-class Dartford boy Mick Jagger), The Kinks were observing the class system sharply in song, taking apart the social mores that still straddled Britain. Ray was all at once laughing at it and seemingly celebrating the quirky nature of what England had come to.

Typically for the Kinks, the song was their biggest hit for some time, re-establishing them right in the epicentre of Brit cool with a song parodying it. It was the sort of situation at which Ray must have allowed himself a smirk. The song also garnered its own controversy when the leering fools on Fleet Street cottoned on to the line "when he pulls his frilly nylon panties right up tight …" A whiff of the cordite of camp had them scuttling to their typewriters in the mock shock outrage so loved of their trade.

It was a far clearer example of the Kinks' camp that had been hinted at in 'See My Friends'. The song also poked fun at the sexual mores that lurked just below the surface of stiff-upper-lip England. It worked on every level. Lyrically barbed, it tore into the hipness of the pop scene and the tight-arsed world of middle England. It took no sides, it took no prisoners, it was hilarious, and it was coupled to a great tune. It was an absolute classic slice of big-beat pop, and a prime example of just how to write a brilliant song, typical of the two-minute vignettes that

Ray was turning out at the time. Awesome. 'Dedicated Follower Of Fashion' was followed up swiftly the next month in some countries by 'A Well Respected Man', which explored the hypocrisy inherent in upper-middle-class society with a great tune sung in Ray's wry voice over a churning acoustic guitar. The well-respected man is all surface; scratch away and a different world appears, a kinkier world. It was the hypocrisy that Ray was railing against.

Meanwhile its author was struggling. Just after the single came out, he had a breakdown. The intense workload and the added pressure of being in The Kinks was just too much for Ray's sensitive psyche, and in a daze, he found himself in Denmark St. trying to punch his press agent, then being chased down the street by the police before being bundled into a taxi and sent to a psychiatrist.

Ray's breakdown gave him a welcome break. It was needed. The time out was well spent and he began to write more new songs. 'End Of the Season' and 'Too Much On my Mind' came together, and then out popped 'Sunny Afternoon'. At that point he knew he'd written a classic. A proper classic. A song that would last forever. On release it was one of the greatest singles of the sixties.

This was a fertile period for Davies. 'I'm Not Like Anybody Else', the B-side of 'Sunny Afternoon', was a perfect expostulation of the yin and yang relationship with his brother Dave. The song, ostensibly a plea for independence by Ray, was sung in the main by Dave and underlined the clash between Dave's more physical presence and Ray's more intellectual art-school inclinations. The song burned with a tension and an innate violence that even the Stones could not match. The Kinks' barely suppressed violence was unmatched by any the

band of the times and not touched on until the punk explosion 10 years later. 'I'm Not Like Anyone Else' was also a plea for independence in the homogenous world of pop. Ray was not the typical pop star. He looked uncomfortable in the photo shoots, and he lacked the dumbness required in the pop world.

The album recorded, The Kinks were back on the road again. Of course, things were not to run smoothly. Pete Quaife was injured in a car crash in Morecambe, meaning he had to be replaced for Top Of The Pops by stand-in John Dalton. Quaife decided not to return to the band, half-recuperating and half-retiring from the intensity and bust-ups of being in The Kinks.

Dalton stepped into the breach. It was bad moment for the band. Quaife was not a songwriter, but had been a key member of the group. He was the one member who everyone got on with, the group's anchorman as well as being a rock-solid bass player. At the same time, they pulled in notorious New York music hustler Alan Klein to renegotiate their contract with Pye.

Pye was paying the band peanuts. It was a typical sixties contract. The notorious Klein tore into the record label, leaving negotiations dragging on for months and delaying the release of Face To Face, which was the best Kinks album yet. With its lead single, 'Sunny Afternoon', at number one, it was left waiting in the wings and missed its moment of glory, a typical fuck-up for the band. On its eventual release in autumn 1966, Face To Face showed the Kinks moving up a creative gear.

Face To Face was the first album that really saw the total flowering of Ray's songwriting talent. Like may other groups of the period, The Kinks had been

recording their live set for albums, with a couple of slower songs thrown in and the odd foray into something a bit more experimental. The Kinks, more than most of their contemporaries, had created some interesting songs. Now they had made a whole album brimming with songwriting brilliance and originality. Face To Face had less foot-to-the-floor guitar riffing, with several of the tracks being hooked around a harpsichord, giving the record a baroque feel, or driven by the acoustic guitar. It would be several years before The Kinks returned to their hard-rock sound.

Whilst The Beatles were cutting their groundbreaking Revolver and showing the first flowerings of their escape from being a beat group, The Kinks were easily keeping up.

> "Then I got together with my brother and a friend and we decided to play dates. The more we played, the more we wanted to do it. And it got to a stage where we wanted to do it all the time."
>
> Ray Davies

Some claim that Face To Face was the first concept album, with the songs being linked together in the form of social observation. The concept album has become a bit of a joke in music circles in recent years, but in the hands of The Kinks it was always brilliantly executed. Ray's background in studying theatre at college and his vibrant imagination were the key. He had certainly been after some kind of continuity on the album, his original idea being to link the songs with sound effects, but Pye stood firm against the idea, making The Kinks deliver the album as a more conventional series of songs.

Whether it was The Kinks or the Pretty Things who came up with the idea of the concept album is a moot point; The Kinks certainly executed the idea best in the coming years. Face To Face was The Kinks' best yet and garnered the band heaps of praise.

Unfortunately, it flopped, only hitting the middle reaches of the chart, the first in series of brilliant albums that somehow slipped through the net. It was a bizarre situation. The band was still having big hit singles and making albums that were cutting edge, as clever and brilliant as The Beatles, but somehow the public just was not latching on. It was the story of The Kinks' career, one of frustrations and bloody-mindedness. Instead of panicking or reverting back to a more conventional sound, Ray just continued on his brilliant, idiosyncratic path. And thank God for that, because what was about to follow were some of the best records of the whole decade.

Not only an absolute Kinks classic, 'Sunny Afternoon' is one of the classic songs by anyone from the sixties, and a song that is as loved now as when it was released. This had everything great about The Kinks in one song, from its fantastic melody to its cutting lyrics and its great use of instrumentation, hooking around the strident acoustic guitar with flourishes of honky-tonk piano. Ray's presentation of a distinctively English voice, in opposition to the more American-influenced vocals of his contemporaries, was the first flowering of a truly English pop music that actually sounded purely English, a form that has been much copied over the years.

The song was released as a single and went to number one for that climactic summer when England won the World Cup. It also knocked The Beatles off the top after only one week, to the eternal satisfaction of its author. It was the perfect moment for the quintessentially English band to come up with the summer anthem for the very week that England won the World Cup – absolute perfect synchronicity.

The songs on the album were:

PARTY LINE (RD Davies)
Sung by Dave, the album opener recounted the narrator's frustration and fascination with the girl who shared his phone connection, now a quaintly dated notion.

ROSY WON'T YOU PLEASE COME HOME (RD Davies)
A plea to one of Ray and Dave's older sisters, who had emigrated to Australia. Ray had lived for a while with Rosy, her husband Arthur and their son Terry. All three family members were to crop up in other Kinks songs.

DANDY (RD Davies)
A US Top-10 hit for Herman's Hermits, this knockabout ditty concerned the amorous exploits of a ladies' man.

TOO MUCH ON MY MIND (RD Davies)

A song of tortured introspection, underlining the pressures that resulted in Ray's breakdown.

SESSION MAN (RD Davies)

An in-joke directed at keyboard player Nicky Hopkins, who was prominent throughout the track. The deliberately tortuous rhymes of "session", "musician" and "chord progression" added to the sense of fun.

RAINY DAY IN JUNE (RD Davies)

Beginning, like several other songs on the album, with a sound effect, this was a sinister evocation of the creatures that emerge after a thunderstorm. Ray explained that the song's genesis occurred when he set out to capture that slightly threatening feel that always occurs just after a thunderstorm. "I love rain and the moistness after a storm", he noted, "and it was about fairies and little evil things within the trees that come to life." With its slow, menacing chord work, this was the work of a band creating a sound sculpture, rather than an organised, traditional song.

HOUSE IN THE COUNTRY (RD Davies)

A track reflecting Ray's fascination with the lifestyles of the rich, which began when the band backed Robert Wace at society events.

HOLIDAY IN WAIKIKI (RD Davies)

Inspired by the band's visit to Hawaii, the song told the story of the English holidaymaker who discovered that Waikiki wasn't all he expected; the grass skirts turned out to be PVC!

MOST EXCLUSIVE RESIDENCE FOR SALE (RD Davies)

A companion piece to both House in the Country and Sunny Afternoon depicting the nouveau riche falling on hard times.

FANCY (RD Davies)

A short acoustic gem with Ray again using the drone-like nature of Indian music to create something remarkable. "I had this silly old Framus guitar", he explained, "that I played on all these records. I had the wrong strings on it. But it had a nice quality. It was a picking sound and it could sustain one note, as Indian music does. The song deals with perception. "Fancy was a remarkable musical excursion, made special by Ray's measured vocal and such hard-hitting lines as 'No one can penetrate me / They only see / What's in their own fancy', which stands as a remarkably succinct summing up of one of the effects of fame. "When I started writing that", he noted, "it was at the time when people really wanted to find out what was wrong with me. All my life I have been able to keep them out."

LITTLE MISS QUEEN OF DARKNESS (RD Davies)

The girl who can have anyone except the boy she really wants.

YOU'RE LOOKIN' FINE (RD Davies)

This second showcase for Dave's singing seemed slight compared to the rest of the album.

SUNNY AFTERNOON (RD Davies)

While the Kinks' album sales were declining, their presence in the singles chart was as strong as ever, as evidenced by Sunny Afternoon, their third (and final) chart-topper.

The Kinks recorded this song, which best summed up their new approach, on Friday the 13th of May 1966. It took them three hours to do so. Ray had bad hay fever, and so could only manage one vocal take. Pye rushed the record out to cash in on the long, hot summer that had been forecast. With its descending piano line, catchy chorus, and striking lyrics, the record sailed into the charts, beautifully

defining the season with its boozy atmosphere and hints of decadence, all of which seemed to tap into a growing consciousness that all was not well in Swinging London. As England lifted the World Cup on the 30th of July 1966, Sunny Afternoon stood at the top of the charts. Ray's reaction? "I wished that I had a machine gun so that I could kill us all and everything would stop there – but we had to get to Exeter for the concert."

I'LL REMEMBER (RD Davies)

A fitting closing track with its air of resigned finality, the song perfectly captured the bittersweet relationship with the past that Davies would mine further.

CHAPTER 7 - SOMETHING ELSE BY THE KINKS

Within a week of the release of Face To Face, The Kinks were back in the studio recording a new single, 'Dead End Street'. It was released two weeks later and was, as Ray explained, a modern day Depression song, a song about people having no way out, a typically cheery subject.

It saw him turning his keen eye away from the upper classes and the dandies in London to the rest of the English public. One of the first great English social commentary pop songs, 'Dead End Street' was a genuine precursor to punk, both lyrically and musically. We can also hear its influence on such bands as Madness and the Jam, with its stark storytelling of the reality of urban Britain. Of course, The Kinks were much too intelligent to write just a straightforward song about tough lives. The song's tune is jaunty and its lyrics are great, like a gritty play for the day, with keen observations and some moments of poignant humour.

As ever, Ray was in a different place than his contemporaries in 1966 swinging London, where there was plenty of drugs and decadence – high times. Instead, Ray would be up in Bradford visiting Rasa's parents and hearing tales of the real world. This fascinated him; this was the world he had grown up in and it attracted his misfit nature. He seemed to love the very idea of doing the opposite to what was hip.

Whilst hip was flouncing around the capital city in a druggy haze, the rest of the UK was in a decidedly different place. Yet again, though, Ray's genius was to write a song that both camps could dig. 'Dead End Street' sounded like the hippest and coolest pop song, a song that would sound right in a hip scene in London or in a brawling northern boozer. It was a blast of reality in a pop scene that was lost in a mist of druggy delusions.

It was like the very first punk song. It was a blast of reality juxtaposed against the decadent utopian dream of the emerging hippies. It saw Ray drawing on his own working-class youth and saw him comment perfectly on the gritty reality of people's lives in a way that his contemporaries never convincingly could.
Like all the classic Kinks songs, 'Dead End Street' oozed cinematic appeal. Just listening to it put a picture in listeners' heads. It made sense that The Kinks were one of the first bands ever to film a pop promo when they made a film to go with the song. The clip showed them walking through Camden carrying a coffin, an idea that Oasis would crib 40 years later for their 'Importance Of Being Idle' video. Unfortunately, back in the sixties, coffins were considered a bit taboo, and the film clip was banned by the BBC.

With some time off from their hectic schedule, The Kinks recorded another couple of singles. The first of these was yet another jaunty, quirky song – and another brilliant tune.

'Mr. Pleasant', released everywhere apart from the UK, is often overlooked in The Kinks' canon because of its follow-up single, the classic 'Waterloo Sunset'. This is a shame, because it's as good as any of their singles during this period. Ray, yet again, sings over a genius, quirky, musical backdrop about the wealthy, this time a hard-working man who has ground his way to the top with his pleasant smile

> I still like to keep tapes of the few minutes before the final take, things that happen before the session. Maybe it's superstitious, but I believe if I had done things differently - if I had walked around the studio or gone out - it wouldn't have turned out that way.

Ray Davies

and has been rewarded with a pleasant life. The sucker punch comes in the third verse, when we find out that Mrs. Pleasant is flirting with a younger man.

Then came 'Waterloo Sunset', one of the greatest pop songs ever released. A song so cinematic and so beautiful it is hard to believe that it is all crammed into less than three minutes of pop bliss. It came to Ray in a dream when he was remembering being extremely ill in hospital as a youth. When he was wheeled outside, so that he could see the Thames after days of being in a stuffy ward, he thought just how romantic the river looked.

At first he had wanted to write about a Liverpool sunset, commenting on the death of Merseybeat, but he felt far more comfortable singing about his own city, his own backdrop. The words came easily, and the tune fell out of his head as he worked it out on the piano after waking up with it in his mind.

The song could only have been written by Ray Davies. It captures a small moment as Terry meets Julie (loosely based on Terence Stamp and Julie Christie) by Waterloo Bridge, a moment detailed in a song that oozes atmosphere and captures the geography and the time perfectly. It's like a painting, a true work of pop art. 'Waterloo Sunset' is an awesome pop song and one that will be played forever by anyone who wants to capture the spirit of that time. 'Waterloo Sunset' was another massive worldwide hit, yet again underlining The Kinks' uncanny ability to write a great pop song that defined the times. The Kinks seemed to be in a great position as 1967 rolled on, but, as ever, the gods were conspiring against them. On the back of 'Waterloo Sunset' they should have been breaking back into the ranks of the top four bands again, but the chance was squandered by uncertain management, litigation, and their own self-destructive attitude.

Pop was moving away from its focus on singles, to albums. Although the Kinks were writing albums that were equal to, if not better than, those of many of the bigger bands, no one seemed to be buying them. Pop was also moving away from the UK to the USA. America had become the epicentre, and any British band worth its salt was touring there or working the American market. Of course, The Kinks had big problems with this, mainly because they were still banned from the USA and had to be content with touring the UK and Europe, thus becoming increasingly marginalised from the heart of pop action. It was in the middle of this gradual slide away from the heartland of pop that Dave Davies stepped out of his brother's shadow. The younger Kink had a massive solo hit with the Dylanesque pathos of 'Death Of Clown', a song that was a plea for peace and quiet from the helter-skelter pop-star life, a bit like John Lennon's 'Help'. 'Death Of A Clown was a huge hit and Dave briefly stepped out of his brother's shadow.

The younger sibling was the glamour side of The Kinks, the closest the band had to a pin-up. He was also the rock 'n' roll heart of the band, its wildest member, famed for his carousing and his wild stage antics as well as for his increasingly eccentric outfits. From day one he had always been the most flamboyant dresser in the band, wearing the knee high boots and having the longest hair in pop music; but by 1967 he was in full regency mode, wearing a regular pied-piper wardrobe complete with a curious Noddy hat and big sideboards. No matter what Dave wore, he always carried it of with panache and verve. He always looked cool. After all, pop stars were meant to dress up, and that mid-sixties regency-dandy look was one of the great looks from the pop pantheon.

Still only 21, Dave looked set to have a big career of his own and recorded a follow-up single called 'Susannah's Still Alive', which was a smaller hit later that year. His single after that, 'Lincoln County', was a flop, and his solo excursion ground to a halt. If things had been handled better by The Kinks' management, or if he'd had the confidence to record a full solo album at that time, he would have probably become a pop star on his own terms, but, as ever, things did not work out that way. The Kinks were also in court fighting over their publishing in a case that ran through to the following year and ended up inconclusively. This didn't help matters.

That summer they returned to the studio to work on their next album, Something Else by the Kinks. The first big change was that Ray had started co-producing, with Shel Tamy sharing the producer's chair. This all made sense, as Ray had produced the previous two Kinks singles and

no one had really noticed, especially Shel Tamy, who had failed to realise that the singer had remixed some of the recent songs after Tamy had left the studio in the evening.

Ray wanted to execute his own vision of The Kinks sound and was getting into the production side of things, a move that he regretted years later, feeling that his production work may have let down some of the songs. In some ways he was right. Song-wise, the album is as good as anything in this period, but something was lacking in the production, which, although it sounds sprightly enough, somehow pales in comparison to The Kinks' contemporaries. Played against a Beatles record, listeners can really see why George Martin was the fifth Beatle in terms of his creative contribution to the band. When he created that sonic backdrop for the Fab Four he had the unerring ability to make the records both sound polished and tingle with the electric excitement of innovation. The Kinks, in comparison, sound smaller and tinnier, although not disastrously so.

Their records do sound fine enough, but they just lack that certain crucial production edge that was basically required to keep up with the Beatles or the other bands that The Kinks should have been level with. Apart from that, the songwriting is again faultless. Ray had hit a groove and come up with yet another set of songs that dragged big meanings from the mundane, or that used characters to explore situations, a series of songs that combined sixties rock 'n' roll with music-hall and a myriad of other styles, and that never let up in the imagination stakes.

The songs on the album were:

DAVID WATTS (RD Davies)

Ray's ode to the perfect schoolboy was actually inspired by a gay promoter the band worked and partied with one memorable night up North. The song was not only daring and forceful and melodic, but also sought to capture that feeling every adolescent boy has for someone older than them at school. The Jam's 1978 version made the song famous, providing a boost to the fortunes of both bands. The Kinks subsequently began playing the song live in a form closer to the Jam's more muscular reading than the original.

DEATH OF A CLOWN (RD Davies/D Davies)

Originally released as a Dave Davies solo single in July 1967, this elegiac, gin-soaked collaboration between the brothers was a Number-Three hit. Ray's wife Rasa, a non-credited backing vocalist on many Kinks records, provided the haunting "la-la-la" bridge.

TWO SISTERS (RD Davies)

A brilliant examination, both musically and lyrically, of Ray's feelings towards his brother, first admitting to jealousy, but then deciding in the end that for all Dave's sexual conquests and outrageous lifestyle, Ray much preferred the quiet life. Casting himself in the role of the dowdy Priscilla, and Dave as the glamorous Sybilla, Ray's songwriting took on new layers of meaning. The lyrics were also inspired by Rasa, and Ray's own six sisters. And who else could have brought in a gorgeous orchestral melody, which is then topped off by a kazoo-like sound? Only Ray Davies.

NO RETURN (RD Davies)

A delicate track with ethereal vocals accompanied by quietly plucked acoustic guitar, No Return has a great Latin tinge to it.

HARRY RAG (RD Davies)

A jaunty celebration of the ordinary cigarette, rather than the herbal variety traditionally favoured by musicians, Harry Rag put us right back in the music hall of Ray's youth, its funny lyrics about tobacco addiction roaring out. Harry Rag is Cockney rhyming slang for fag (cigarette).

TIN SOLDIER MAN (RD Davies)

Marching brass decorated a suburban tale about a slightly pathetic, military-fixated character.

SITUATION VACANT (RD Davies)

A vignette which saw a scheming mother-in-law engineer the break-up of her daughter's marriage.

LOVE ME TILL THE SUN SHINES (RD Davies)

Dave Davies provided the counterpoint to his brother's observational work in typically direct fashion. The song first appeared on the B-side of Death Of A Clown.

LAZY OLD SUN (RD Davies)

As a chronicler of the English summer, Ray was without parallel; here the parched, lethargic atmosphere conjured up a hot day. This was one of the few times the band attempted psychedelia; of course, they did it masterfully.

AFTERNOON TEA (RD Davies)

Romance blossoms, then withers over tea. Who else but Ray Davies would have tackled such subject matter during the Summer of Love?

FUNNY FACE (D Davies)

The rowdy flip side of Dave's less successful second single, Susannah's Still Alive, this interrupted the sequence of quintessentially English songs.

END OF THE SEASON (RD Davies)

"An odd little ballad", according to its composer, End of the Season mourned the passing of summer in the manner of a contemporary Noel Coward. A striking lament.

WATERLOO SUNSET (RD Davies)

Ray later recalled that the song came to him in his sleep and that he heard it as a jazz swing number before placing it within its pop context. One of English pop's most beloved singles, Waterloo Sunset was originally about the death of Merseybeat, before Ray, characteristically, found his muse closer to home when his attention, as ever, wandered backwards. He recalled the time that he had stayed in St. Thomas's hospital on the Embankment as a child. One day, a nurse had wheeled him out onto a balcony which afforded him a spectacular view of Waterloo Bridge, and the idea of writing a great London song took hold. So certain was he of the song's potency, he kept refining it on a regular basis.

CHAPTER 8 - VILLAGE GREEN PRESERVATION SOCIETY

Bizarrely, when considering just how good the songs were on Something Else, it petered out in the charts, peaking at number 35. In America it did even worse, not being helped by the continuing ban, which left the band virtually invisible in the USA. The changing face of pop was not helping, either, with the scene becoming freakier and more far out. As the rest of the scene went into outer space, the Kinks just became more and more English, which, with hindsight, made them seem even more psychedelic than the tripped-out bands.

While most pop songs were, by this time, about freak-outs and tripping, the new Kinks single, 'Autumn Almanac' was about a gardener content with his lot, every winter sweeping up his leaves and putting them in his sack. It was a song about a traditional life, roast beef on Sunday and holidays in Blackpool, a real slice of traditional English life that was not disappearing into a psychedelic horizon, but which was actually still going on in most of the country.

The single, with its horn-driven melody, had Ray wishing it could be covered by a brass band. You can hear the rainy-day ordinariness of real life crackling out of the tune. Not only traditional, it also had a reversed middle section where the tapes were flipped over backwards for a twist. Backwards loops, bending sound out of shape and running it backwards on records, were something that was in vogue at the time. It worked well. With 'Dead End Street' it was a crafty nod to the freakier edge of pop, right in the middle of a traditional pop song. Only an art-school mind like Ray Davies's could have pulled this trick off. This was the end of the mid-sixties Kinks. They would, at this point, take some time off to get on with life.

After a six-month layoff they came back with a new single, the almost effetely camp 'Wonderboy', a song that makes a virtue of its slipshod nature and which was John Lennon's favourite Kinks single. The lyrics were about childhood trying to make sense of those precious years before real life creeps in and kills all the innocence, an innocence that matched the prevailing acid-tinged mood of people like Lennon.

'Wonderboy' was a flop, stalling at number 35 in the charts. It was their first single not to go top-10 since before 'You Really Got Me'. The accompanying tour saw the despondent band getting blown off the stage by the Tremoloes most nights. The two EPs that had been released to capitalise on the tour had also stiffed. There was a general feeling between the band management and the tour promoters that The Kinks' glory days were over and that, maybe, it was time to pack it in.

THE KINKS UNCUT 50 YEARS ON THE ROAD

The band, though, were made of sterner stuff and hit back with their next single 'Days', one of their classics. A complex examination of human relationships, 'Days' not only had a fantastic melody, it also looked at the way that every relationship is dominated by the brooding thought of parting, suggesting that loss is at the heart of them all. Although not reaching number one, 'Days' put the Kinks back into the upper reaches of the charts. Meanwhile, Dave's career was foundering, with his third single, the driving 'Lincoln County', not charting. Even though it was a killer single, sometimes in pop music the gods stop smiling and the hits dry up. The history of pop music is littered with great,

lost records, records that should have made it, and 'Lincoln County' is one of those. It would be years before he got enough confidence to finish off his solo album.

Meanwhile Ray had been stockpiling the songs that would eventually come out as Village Green Preservation Society, an album that was even further removed from the pop Zeitgeist than anything they had recorded before. It was an album that harked back to a vintage England, and sounded like a celebration of a world gone by. With Ray firmly in the producer's chair and in total control, in addition to writing all the songs, it was

the first Kinks album to see the band veer closer to being a Ray Davies project than a full band workout.

Pete Quaife had returned to the fold and was temporarily back on bass for one last stand, as The Kinks gave up on being hip and contemporary and disappeared into a world of their own. The resulting album was one of the best releases of the sixties, and was naturally their worst-selling record.

Written by Ray when he was in a depressed state after his nervous breakdown, the album's first song, 'Village Green', had been written back in 1966. Ray explained it as being about 'a mystical place', a long-lost England that he could escape to, his own version of Never Never Land, his own personal Land of Oz. It set the agenda for the whole album, The Kinks' first fully realised concept album, stuffed full of characters and sketches. It was meant to be Ray's version of Dylan Thomas's 'Under Milk Wood', a brilliantly worked out concept that may not have sold at the time but which has become one of the most cherished albums of the period. At one point, Ray even thought of presenting it as a stage play. The whole album has a melancholic feel to it, an otherworldly take on a reality that never was. It is a childlike look at a world gone by, a vision of England that was unique. It is also a long-lost work of total genius. Few albums can have been as perfect as this.

Village Green Preservation Society had a troubled birth, being scrapped and re-recorded. Ray laboured over it till the last minute. His vision was unique. Typically, he later claimed that he should never have been allowed to release it in the first place. Thank God he persevered, because listening to it years later, it sounds fantastic. A cycle of songs, each one a gem, it became a cult album that few bought at the time, but which is now considered to be one of the great albums of the period.

Much of the material had originally been written for a potential Ray Davies solo album or for a stage play, because Ray was unsure whether the songs would fit into The Kinks' canon. Ostensibly, the band was moving away from the hit-single formula that had been their lifeblood, but listening to the album now it seems peppered with singles, from 'Big Sun' to the witty shots of 'People Take Pictures Of Each Other' to the driving 'Johnny Thunder' and the sing-along 'Starstruck'.

Originally planned as a two-album boxed set, Pye pegged back the band's ambitions, eventually releasing the 15-track version. By the time Village Green Preservation Society had come out on November the 22nd 1968 – the same day as the Beatles' White Album – The Kinks were so far out of sync that it had no chance of being a hit. The industry did not consider them revolutionary enough to be underground, and they were too intelligent to be bubblegum, leaving them high and dry. One of the best pop bands of their period having just released an album of brilliant pop material, they were left with a withered fan base. It is a sad indictment of the inanity and the pointlessness of pop that an album as brilliant as this was left foundering. And foundering was the key word. The band were even booked in to play cabaret gigs in the north of England, an ignominious defeat for a band that was always being chewed up and spat out by the music business.

Being banned from the States had been a creative bonus for them. They were left to their own creative devices and chronicled the aspirations and foibles of their fellow countrymen.

By 1968 they had become the quintessentially English rock group, concerned with writing about the lives of ordinary people with extraordinary insight, making the mundane glamorous.

It was a neat trick and one at which Ray excelled with a brilliant, willful eccentricity. Village Green Preservation Society made a strong case for Ray Davies to be the Poet Laureate.

He had the same magical touch of the poetically mundane as John Betjeman, the same way of picking out the small details of life and investing them with meaning and a power.

Although the album disappeared at the time, it has always remained on the catalogue. People have bought it in a constant stream, and it is now The Kinks' best-selling, non-compilation album. Ray pertinently referred to it recently as the "most successful flop of all time."

The songs on the album were:

THE VILLAGE GREEN PRESERVATION SOCIETY (RD Davies)
Along with its companion piece, Village Green, the title track, was nostalgia in undiluted form, presenting a vision of an England which, if it ever existed, was rapidly disappearing. Odd then that the very American Donald Duck should have been the first candidate for preservation…

DO YOU REMEMBER WALTER (RD Davies)
Nostalgia was tempered by a realisation that the past can never be recaptured, as demonstrated in this bittersweet lament to lost schoolboy friendship.

PICTURE BOOK (RD Davies)
Similarly, photographs only serve as reminders that the past is gone forever.

JOHNNY THUNDER (RD Davies)
An archetypal Ray Davies character – the rebel motorbiker who never quite managed to leave his home town.

LAST OF THE STEAM-POWERED TRAINS (RD Davies)

Ray reflected on feelings of personal, and, judging by The Kinks' declining record sales, professional obsolescence via the metaphor of steam trains.

BIG SKY (RD Davies)

A classic chorus wound out of the spoken verses of this reflection on the insignificance of everyday problems in the greater scheme of things.

SITTING BY THE RIVERSIDE (RD Davies)

One of The Kinks' marvellously languid odes to lazing around, sung in an almost ridiculously mannered way.

ANIMAL FARM (RD Davies)

The song's narrator imagined sanctuary from the madness of the real world, in the country, amongst animals.

VILLAGE GREEN (RD Davies)

Recorded some months earlier than the rest of the album, this track provided the starting point for the concept, and was the purest statement of the album's theme. The Village Green represented a safer, happier past, and a refuge from the pressures of stardom.

STARSTRUCK (RD Davies)

A warning about the tricks that fame can play, not only on the star but also on those around him.

PHENOMENAL CAT (RD Davies)

The dark fairytale of a supernatural moggy, which was both unsettling and amusing.

ALL OF MY FRIENDS WERE THERE (RD Davies)

Drink-related, onstage embarrassment in a piece that evoked the music hall, particularly in Ray's comical delivery.

WICKED ANNABELLA (RD Davies)

Dave sang this flirtation with the stylistic trappings of psychedelia – distorted vocals and disjointed drums underpinned the story of a wicked witch.

MONICA (RD Davies)

A naïve and touching declaration of love to a lady of the night.

PEOPLE TAKE PICTURES OF EACH OTHER (RD Davies)

Ray's aversion to family snapshots as futile attempts to capture the past, closed the album with elegant wit.

> "What I try to do probably doesn't come out. What I've worked out what I do - I might not be right - is to do something very personal, and then suddenly I look at it, up in the air. I blow it up and look at it and then I come down again - a better man.

Ray Davies

CHAPTER 9 – ARTHUR (OR THE DECLINE AND FALL OF THE BRITISH EMPIRE)

Entering 1969, The Kinks seemed like yesterday's men. Pop had passed them by. No matter what kind of creative high they were on, their records were not selling and they were, as mentioned, reduced to playing a series of cabaret gigs.

It was an ignoble fall from grace. They were stood down on the sidelines. There were, though, projects to be undertaken; among them was writing the soundtrack for an hour-long play for Granada, called Arthur. Ray was working on a screenplay with Julian Mitchell. The film, however, was eventually scrapped.

There was also to be another project, with Ray writing a song a week for another TV production starring Eleanor Bron.

Ray's creativity was now reaching fever pitch. The Kinks released their next single, 'Plastic Man', which was pulled by the BBC when it was just starting to climb the charts, because it had the word 'bum' in the lyrics. Outrageous! The song featured Ray singing in another of his voices, this time the chirpy cockney, in a song about a man made out of, er, plastic.

Ray later admitted the single was rushed out to go with a tour the Kinks were about to embark on in 1969. He now claims he preferred the B-side, 'King Kong', which is an odd piece of work, an almost neo-glam anthem four years before glam held sway. 'King Kong' has a flavour of T. Rex to it, and the sort of vocal that Marc Bolan would make his own when he was in his pomp.

> " When you are making a record and if you spend too much time over it, you have to record it a tone lower or cut the tones lower because you can't reach some of the notes, I find this. But when you go on stage, you have to put the key up and it really changes the whole thing. "
>
> Ray Davies

The new album, Arthur (Or the Decline and Fall of the British Empire), was released in late 1969 and saw The Kinks develop the concept album idea still further. Whereas Village Green had been a collection of songs based around a theme, or a feeling, this was an album of songs built around a story line from Ray's childhood. It was based on the experiences of the Davies's brother-in-law Arthur, who, like many Brits in the sixties, emigrated to Australia. Arthur was a carpet layer and struggled to find work in the early-sixties UK, so he moved halfway around the world in search of the better life.

The album was a history lesson, a slice of contemporary life. The song cycle described the England that Arthur once knew, the promise of a better life in Australia that bewitches the Brits, the resolve of the British in World War Two, and the death of Arthur's brother in the previous war. It was a keen piece of social observation from Ray, who was again refusing to propagate the sixties' myth. The album touches on the concerns of the post-war generation with such songs as the classic 'Shangri La', one of the great Kinks songs, which was about the superficiality of Arthur's home. 'Shangri La' was another Kinks single that should have been a hit but wasn't.

There is a touch of the old England in the album, but this time it's not the mystical Village Green but a decaying England, an England of lost dreams and lack of direction, the real England and not the England of Ray's dreams. A series of songs about the England that was disappearing into modernity, Arthur… hangs together as a whole piece.

The concept album is a much-maligned form. Most them were eventually fairly shallow pieces about elves and magic castles, unimaginative tosh, but in the hands of The Kinks they were excellent mini plays,

like kitchen-sink-drama films. Arthur… brought all of Ray's songwriting themes – class, family, and the confused morass of a post-war British society that was going through the fastest social upheaval since the industrial revolution – into a sharp and eloquent focus, pulling them together and giving them a personal touch. A dose of roots realism in a rock world that was slowly moving from psychedelic to grassroots blues to prog, all the time pretending and faking it, whilst Ray was singing of reality, an urban England that he made sound dingy and romantic.

The album also saw a return to the stripped-down rock of earlier years, especially on the opening track and single, 'Victoria'. Gone were Nicky Hopkins's keyboards (a shame, as they had been such a crucial feature in the previous few years, but it was time to move on). The songwriting was concise and the playing was tight.

Just before Arthur… had been released, the Kinks were finally allowed back into America. They found a country where things had changed drastically from the innocent days of the beat boom. At the tail-end of the sixties America was in the hangover from the hippie era. The Vietnam War and the anti-war demonstrations were in full swing, and pop had turned into rock. Instead of being big news, co-heading with the Beach Boys at the Hollywood Bowl on their last tour, the band were now supporting Spirit in far smaller venues. They found themselves staying in cheap hotels and shopping at the local supermarkets for food. It was a real grassroots tour, a real comedown for a band with 17 hit singles in the UK.

The Americans may have been enthralled with Englishness, but their idea of England was a long way away from the Davies version. The American England was the England of pop bands taking

American music and selling it back; a real coals-to-Newcastle version composed of cranking up the blues, putting an English gloss on it and selling it back across the pond, a process started, ironically, by The Kinks themselves with 'You Really Got Me'!

The Kinks' idiosyncratic, highly localised take on little England was enthralling to pockets of fans; they had become the ultimate cult band – the first ever indie band. Their world view made little sense in the general scheme of things. Their first tour back in the States was the start of a 10-year graft by the band back up the ladder.

An ambitious multimedia project, Arthur… pushed forward the boundaries of just what a rock album could be, its relative lack of success proving just how backwards rock had become despite its avowed interest in moving forward. If there was going to be no space for The Kinks in the mainstream, then rock's claim that it was smart and challenging seemed hollow. In reality, the sixties were petering out into a load of denim and boogie, fake messiahs, and watered versions of the greats. There was simply to be no room at the inn for a band as smart as The Kinks.

Before they toured America there was also a little matter of getting another bass player. Three days after the album's release and just before the American tour, Pete Quaife finally left The Kinks. He claimed that he was fed up with playing "pretty bubblegum music" and tired of playing simplistic bass lines. There was no enmity in his departure, but there was an air of frustration at being stifled by Ray Davies. Quaife had been the band's spokesman in the early days. Ray had been far too repressed for things like that and Dave far too wild, so it had often been left to the bass player's wit and humour to deal with the interviews.

Quaife's departure was the end of The Kinks as a band proper. It also marked the end of the first part of their career. If the band had split at this point, their reputation would have remained in rock circles as the coolest band of the sixties, with a perfect catalogue and their artistic integrity intact. Instead, they brought back John Dalton on bass and finally, on re-entering the States, adapted their sound to breaking the key record market in the world.

The songs on the album were:

VICTORIA (RD Davies)
Ray's slurred vocals made the lyrics to the opening verse difficult to distinguish, as Arthur proclaimed his love for and loyalty to the Empire. Victoria was the third single from the album and a minor success at 33. It also provided a rare brush with the singles chart for the Fall in 1988.

YES SIR, NO SIR (RD Davies)
Both sides of the class divide were laid bare, from the unthinking deference to authority of the working-class soldiers to the callous indifference of the officers in the stunning middle section.

SOME MOTHER'S SON (RD Davies)
An eloquent, understated anti-war song; like the previous track, it detailed Arthur's experiences in the Great War.

DRIVIN' (RD Davies)
Some light relief, set in a time when a drive in the country could still be a relaxing way of escaping the pressures of life.

BRAIN WASHED (RD Davies)
An abrupt change of mood for this angry attack on the system and those beaten down by it. The brass section added punch to the sentiments.

AUSTRALIA (RD Davies)

Inspired by the real-life Arthur's decision to leave England for the promise of a better life in the New World, the song ended with a lengthy, quasi-psychedelic instrumental coda.

SHANGRI LA (RD Davies)

Arthur's own empire was a modest house called Shangri La. The picture of claustrophobic suburbia was reinforced as the neighbours "say their lines", giving the impression of being trapped in a play. Released as a single to coincide with the album, Shangri La's three-part structure and five-minute length effectively prevented it from gaining enough airplay to dent the charts.

MR CHURCHILL SAYS (RD Davies)

Churchill's famous speech provided the background for the Blitz as the ordinary man prepared to make sacrifices for the war effort..

SHE BOUGHT A HAT LIKE PRINCESS MARINA (RD Davies)

Something of a return to music-hall territory (including a silly kazoo part), the song depicted celebrity-worship as an escape from the grim realities of life. Princess Marina had been a popular member of the Royal Family, something of a pre-war equivalent of Lady Diana.

YOUNG AND INNOCENT DAYS (RD Davies)

This largely acoustic lament for lost youth elegantly restated a familiar Davies theme.

NOTHING TO SAY (RD Davies)

One of Arthur's sons reflected on the gulf between generations.

ARTHUR (RD Davies)

The album ended in an upbeat, almost anthemic mode with a tribute to its titular hero, the ordinary man who has watched his beloved Empire fall apart.

APTER 10 – LOLA VERSUS POWERMAN
D THE MONEYGOROUND, PART ONE

ur… had sold better than Village Green
servation Society, but it hardly set the charts
nt. The Kinks were, as ever, in a curious
ition. They were the outsiders, making some of
cleverest records of their period, but apart from
ult crowd no one was interested.

hits were drying up, but at least they were
k in America where they were touring hard and
ting a loyal cult following. With Ray now firmly at
helm, the band's creative ideas were unfettered,
the concepts were becoming grander. Arthur…
shown a vision that no other band at the time
ld match.

y had made a rock opera that was wordy, smart,
filmic without being pretentious or embarrassing,
ch was quite a trick, as other groups had found
, and they were about to set out on another
cept from the bursting mind of Ray Davies.

he meantime, Dave was in the studio trying to
sh his solo album. Typically, he had missed the
it. His brief solo success had been two years
ore, but he'd shelved the songs he'd been
ording, like 'Shoemakers Daughter', 'Are You
ady Girl?', 'Mr. Reporter', 'Do You Wish To Be A
n?', and 'Groovy Movies', as he felt the project
be too rushed and not ready. This was a shame,
bootlegs reveal there was a cool album sitting
re. Reality was slapping the band around the
e everywhere they turned in the cruel world of
b. They were in a tumble from grace, a Spinal
p-style slide from the top. The only European tour
y could get was in the small clubs in Sweden,
uding a gig in an amusement park, a sideshow
a fake Disney world. It was a bottoming-out.

Then there was the American tour. There was much
work to be done. The band had been away for
far too long. Their initial massive success of three
huge hits had petered out into the occasional hit
with 'Sunny Afternoon', and then misses like 'Mr.
Pleasant' and, astonishingly, 'Waterloo Sunset',
which did not do anything in the States. Their
albums had been left to become cult curios. The
crowd they had, though, was immensely loyal,
hanging onto every word, singing along with the
intensity of a cult audience.

In mainstream terms, the Kinks just did not fit into
America any more than England. They were not cute
enough for the pop press, they were not outrageous
enough for the boys, and they were not interesting
enough for the already celebrity-lifestyle-obsessed
media. They played up their ordinariness, and the
closest they had to a genuine rock star was Dave
Davies.

The mainstream media shunned them, and their
records were becoming increasingly hard to find.
Conversely, though, the newly emerging underground
press was backing them to the hilt. Magazines like
Crawdaddy and Rolling Stone printed critics who
began to praise their concept albums to the hilt, and
it was in this underground, the centre of the emerging
post-hippie scene, that The Kinks were being lauded
when their plane touched down for their American
return. They arrived on the crest of a mini-wave,
with rave reviews of the Arthur album and some real
grassroots excitement at their return, a cult band with
their battered backline and reputations enthralling
the fierce and partisan crowds who turned up to see
them perform.

In Chicago they supported the Who. It was a lesson
in just what America wanted from a British rock band.
The Who were powerful and bombastic, they had

been constantly touring the States for three years and were the comfortable headliners over a band they used to support back in the UK. Pete Townsend, a life-long supporter of The Kinks, still raved about them. What the Who had to offer America in their explosiveness, however, was everything that the Kinks could not.

The Who had also just released Tommy, and were getting all the kudos for coming up with the idea of the concept album, even though The Kinks had done it first. When Arthur... limped out six months later, it was seen as being very much an anticlimax.
Trumped by their old mates, The Kinks had yet again lost their moment of glory. Despite their album being far superior musically, lyrically, and narratively to what the Who had delivered, its themes were too homely and too real.

The Who were breaking into the super league whilst The Kinks were left floundering around. The Kinks were perceived to be copying the Who, which must have been galling, since Ray had been years ahead of their old mockers.

The lack of success for Arthur... was a blow to the band. It had been really well thought out and they had given it their best shot, but it had just not broken through. Of the three singles released from the album, the laconic 'Drivin' and the genius 'Shangri La' were inexplicably flops, whilst 'Victoria' garnered minor chart status. It was tough going, the only respite being that the album had sold more than Village Green Preservation Society.

They had two more American tours in still smaller venues. It was tough going. Touring America at that level always is, and the touring party had resorted to a drunken despondency. They were literally dying on their feet despite being at a creative peak.

They needed something fast to resolve the situation. And that something was 'Lola'.

Just when it seemed that The Kinks had completely run out of steam, just when it seemed that they had used up their canon of classic songs, Ray came up with what became perhaps their most famous song. 'Lola' was based on a drunken night when former manager Robert Wace had danced with a transvestite. He'd been too pissed to care. Ray took the incident, and with that deft campness that was so key to some of his major songwriting triumphs, turned the story into a triumph of sexual innuendo and gender bending, years before this became the norm in pop culture.

They went in to record 'Lola'. Wace said that all the song needed was something that really caught the ear at the beginning, something that The Kinks had been so adept at in the old days of 'You Really Got Me', some simple shots of guitar, maybe? Ray came back with those distinctive chords for the intro and the song was complete. Driven by the simple strumming acoustic guitar, the song is deceptively basic. 'Lola' is one of those great pop sing-along songs, like 'Hey Jude'. It is the kind of song that a football crowd could get its tonsils around if it was not for the risqué subject matter. How they managed to slip a song about smooching with transvestites under the conservative radar of the BBC still raises a smile.

'I'm Ray Davies... and I'm dying.'

Ray Davies

The BBC was more concerned with the reference to "Coca-Cola" and had them re-record it as "cherry cola". Ray had to fly back from New York just to change that one word in the song.

The wordplay in 'Lola' is pure genius, hilarious; it is clever and camp and plays it for laughs. David Bowie turned the taboos touched on into a whole career in the years to come, and they became the norm in the time of the new romantics. As usual, Ray Davies and the Kinks had been there and done it years before anyone else, yet another glorious first in a career littered with innovation.

'Lola' was the first pop song in the three years since homosexuality had been legalised in Britain, to deal with what was still a taboo subject. The twisting and turning nature of the lyrics leave the listener unsure whether Lola is a masculine woman or a feminine man or a transvestite, a piece of gender confusion that sets the tone. The single went top-10 on both sides of the Atlantic, bringing the band a whole new audience and changing the on-stage persona of Ray Davies from awkward chronicler of a dying England to a rabble-rouser, leading the crowd through tongue-in-cheek sing-alongs. The success of 'Lola' and the return to the more extroverted arena of touring America was changing the whole nature of the band.

'Lola' was also the debut of the first permanent Kinks keyboard player. John Gosling, who turned up at the session with long hair and a cape, was swiftly nicknamed 'John The Baptist' by the incredulous band. Gosling auditioned by playing along with the song, and was surprised to hear his first take finally used on the track, but that was the ad hoc nature of The Kinks and something that he would have to get used to in the following years.

Reinvigorated, the band set to work on an album called Lola versus Powerman and the Moneygoround. The concept this time was the highs and lows of the music business, loosely based on their own experiences. It was a cautionary story about a filthy industry. It was The Kinks fighting back.

The songs on this album were:

THE CONTENDERS (RD Davies)

After a short, country-tinged introduction, this turned into a breezy opener driven along by new boy John Gosling's boogie-woogie piano and Dave's blues-rock guitar. Lyrically, The Contenders detailed the desire to succeed and the hunger for fame that drives every aspiring musician, and how this leads to a choice of music over a conventional career. The die was cast …

STRANGERS (D Davies)

The first of Dave's two contributions, Strangers was an enigmatic song that appeared to have no thematic link with the remainder of the album. A memorable, poignant ballad based mainly on piano and acoustic guitar, its charming, understated quality made this something of a hidden gem.

DENMARK STREET (RD Davies)

An exposé of the hypocrisy of music publishers, this harked back stylistically to The Kinks of several years before. Its upbeat, vaudeville ambience masked a vitriolic attack on the mores of the middleman, hedging his bets as he said, 'I hate your music and your hair is too long, but I'll sign you up because I'd hate to be wrong.'

GET BACK IN LINE (RD Davies)

One of the most underrated songs in The Kinks catalogue, this powerful and affecting song not only had relevance in the context of the album, but had a deeper resonance for Ray Davies himself.

As Ray later revealed, his father had experienced long periods of unemployment and found the indignity of having to stand in line to collect his dole money, enormously embarrassing. He had always stated that he didn't want anyone to see him in the dole queue, and the image had obviously stuck in his son's mind.

In terms of the album, this song expressed the feeling of helplessness experienced by aspiring musicians in the face of the power wielded by the Musicians' Union, who had the final say over who would fill all vacancies.

LOLA (RD Davies)

One of the band's best-known numbers, Lola was a hit on both sides of the Atlantic, reaching Number Two in the UK, and even making a brief appearance in the US Top 10.

There are still arguments over its real meaning, and the lyrics flirted with sexual ambiguity before Glam-rock popularised such themes, but in the end, the only thing that matters is that this was a great song with an irresistible melody and an unforgettable hook.

TOP OF THE POPS (RD Davies)

Over an infectious musical backing designed to parody the overtly commercial style normally associated with TV's Top Of The Pops, Ray took a wry look at the way life changes when success finally arrives. As the protagonist's latest single climbed the chart, he found himself suddenly in demand for interviews, surrounded by friends he never knew he had, and being told by his agent that he'd known he'd make it all along.

THE MONEYGOROUND (RD Davies)

A Cockney knees-up that concealed a bitter sideswipe at all the middlemen who make a living out of taking their cut from the income generated by artists. Name checking several former Kinks managers, Ray complained that he'd ended up with "half of goodness knows what" and despaired of ever being able to step off the treadmill to enjoy the fruits of his labour.

THIS TIME TOMORROW (RD Davies)

One of many songs in The Kinks' catalogue lamenting the emptiness of life on the road, this developed from a loose country-rock beginning into a classic mid-tempo number graced by some fine vocal harmonies.

A LONG WAY FROM HOME (RD Davies)

Almost certainly the weakest song on the album, A Long Way From Home had the star's childhood friends and family reflecting on the way fame had changed him and providing him with a timely reminder that he should never forget his roots. Despite Ray's customary sharp observations, A Long Way From Home fell some way short of being memorable, without either a strong melody or a notable hook, and marked the low-point of this collection.

RATS (D Davies)

The second Dave Davies song on the album, Rats was a vicious indictment of the corporate mentality, or the "pin-stripe mind", as the song had it, delivered over a blistering heavy-metal backing.

APEMAN (RD Davies)

Another manifestation of Ray's scepticism of modern technology and the so-called advances it brings to society. Here, he simply wanted to escape the whole sorry mess and return to a simpler lifestyle, laying the blame for the ills of modern society squarely on people's apparent belief that we are above nature, not part of it.

POWERMAN (RD Davies)

On the face of it, Powerman was another song about corruption within the music business, but its contempt for the attitude that power and wealth engender had far wider implications.

GOT TO BE FREE (RD Davies)

The closing number was a modest country-rock song that reiterated Ray's desire to break free of the constraints of life in the music business and of life in general. It was, perhaps, a slight anti-climax after a generally stronger collection of songs, but remained pleasant enough.

> Money and corruption are ruining the land, crooked politicians betray the working man, pocketing the profits and treating us like sheep, and we're tired of hearing promises that we know they'll never keep.
>
> Ray Davies

CHAPTER 11 - MUSWELL HILLBILLIES

With 'Lola' a massive international hit, the Kinks should have been on a roll, but this was a band that somehow always seemed to shoot itself in its collective foot. The follow up single, 'Apeman', had also been a top-five hit, and the album sniffed around the lower reaches of the top 40 in the USA, whilst yet again disappearing in the UK.

It seemed like The Kinks were doomed to be a singles band forever, despite – or because of – their writing complex and fascinating albums complete with their own storylines. At least the Americans were beginning to take notice.

When they should have been promoting the album full-on, Ray became distracted by writing the soundtrack for a film called Percy. Percy was the band's last release for Pye records and disappeared without trace. The album was a bit of an anomaly. The tracks were mainly instrumentals, but there were a handful of songs, not enough for the album to be considered part of The Kinks' proper discography, but rather more of a side project. Professionally, there were chinks in The Kinks' armour. wThe management team had not been over-enamoured with the theme of Lola versus Powerman and the Moneygoround.

With the direct lyrics on 'Moneygoround', how could they be? An album that is cynical about the music industry was bound to hurt their management team. In truth, The Kinks and Wace and Collins had been working together for a long time, and a band as volatile and unpredictable as The Kinks was a hell of a handful for anyone. No surprise, then, that the two parties were beginning to drift apart.

Ironically, the album's top-40 placing in the USA put them back into the frame of the business that they professed to hate. It was beginning to be clear that the band's future was going to be in America, but there would be a few pitfalls before any of that came to fruition.

The rest of the year had been frustrating. There were plans to make Lola versus Powerman and the Moneygoround, Part Two and another album called Songs I Did For Auntie. Both stalled at their initial stages and never came to fruition.

The Kinks' contract with Pye being up, and the recent success of 'Lola' saw them being chased by several labels. Eventually they went to RCA because they felt that they needed a worldwide label with some oomph. The Kinks were now thinking of breaking into America. The ban at last being lifted meant that they were touring hard in the States. Their recent American successes saw them spend more and more time there. Their sixties songs, which for the most part had not been huge hits in the States, were being dug up and reconsidered by critics as masterpieces. They were already seen as one of the key bands from the sixties, a band whose influence far outstripped their record sales.

"No one can penetrate me. They only see what's in their own fancy, always.

Ray Davies

America was changing The Kinks. Ray was no longer the edgy, uncomfortable presence that he had been in the sixties, although this had been part of his charm then. He had become instead, a full-on frontman, a skinny, beanpole, Jaggeresque figure with all the arse-waving theatricals associated with the Stones' frontman. It was a big shift in his stage style. Having become a big, camp, loon with the music-hall styling of a classic rock 'n' roll frontman, Ray had suddenly blossomed into an excellent performer – a most unlikely frontman.

Ray was fast emerging as the most dominant member of the band. Whilst Dave started to drift away from the limelight, his older brother was writing everything, producing on the new sessions, and had, by that time, started managing the band, as they had finally split from the management team that had been with them since the start. The Pye deal over, they signed to RCA and set up their own studio in Hornsey. Ray was in total control and his head was spinning with concepts. Free from the pressure of being in a singles band, he was thinking in terms of bigger concepts with more filmic ideas. There was, however, a danger developing that The Kinks were totally overextending themselves. Meanwhile, RCA was backing them to the hilt. It saw them as one of its main bands, along with David Bowie. The Kinks were one of the two projects the label was keen to get behind.

Released in November 1971, the first album that The Kinks delivered to RCA was Muswell Hillbillies, a record that saw them switch direction yet again. Moving away from their harder-sounding previous album, they produced a more rootsy feel, tinged with country and western and Americana, albeit with a distinctly English twist. It was a completely British, almost cabaret, take on American culture.

The songs are less like stories than Ray had been writing up until then. Rather, the concept is in the themes that make up the songs, which tie the album together. They turned in a downbeat album about the reality of working-class England, a paranoid schizophrenic album of isolation and alcohol, an album about the stresses of modern life and the craving for escape.

Muswell Hillbillies has been described as the sound of madness. Its songs touch on alcoholism, the stress of modern life, schizophrenia, intuitionism, anorexia, and madness – and that's just the first five songs! Somehow, though, Ray made the difficult subject matter into songs that can be sung along to, being a true craftsmen at a new peak in his powers. The album obviously meant a lot to Ray, who used many of the song titles for his chapter headings in his autobiography, X Ray, 20-odd years later.

This was Ray Davies doing his own soul-searching, going back to his roots, and seeing how this affected his life. It was a concept album about his own disaffection with the world, with lyrics that were both soul-searching and coloured with a sense of humour.

The album's title comes from Ray remembering when the Davies family moved to Muswell Hill with all their furniture piled up high on the back of a truck. His filmic mind remembered it like an episode of The Beverley Hillbillies, the American comedy show about a family of rednecks who strike oil and move to Beverly Hills, complete with all their redneck trappings. It did not take much to switch the title around to a more homely one.

Ray deliberately slurred his vocals on it, as the band took on the pretend role of a saloon band playing round the pubs of north London. The Kinks were a million miles away from the jet set world of their contemporaries; the album's cover saw them sitting in a boozer looking down at heel. It's a brilliant sleeve, all atmospheric – a smoky barroom with The Kinks looking very much at home in it. At a time when bands were either glam rock-brickies dressed in tin foil or were away with the fairies playing prog rock, only The Kinks could bring things back down to earth and have themselves photographed looking scruffy in a north London pub – actually the Archway Tavern, two miles away from Muswell Hill.

Muswell Hillbillies was another critical success that failed to chart high, its sales being moderate. Maybe Ray's decision not to write another hit like 'Lola' had much to do with this. Perhaps the subject matter was too downbeat for an audience hoping for more 'Lola'-style sing-alongs. For the purists, this was the last great classic Kinks album – a run of releases that had started with Face To Face. Following Muswell Hillbillies, the concepts would come thick and fast over a few years of Ray Davies being in creative overload, each album seemingly selling less in the UK whilst inching up more sales in America. It was to be a four-year spell of theatrical ideas and overreaching concepts. This was followed by five years of big bucks success in the States with a simplified, stripped-down, rock Kinks.

The songs on the album were:

20TH CENTURY MAN (RD Davies)
In a song lamenting modernisation, the relentless march of technology, and the loss of traditional values, Ray complained of being "… born in a welfare state, ruled by bureaucracy." This strong, upbeat opener had a bouncy backing track and featured a spirited vocal performance.

ACUTE SCHIZOPHRENIA PARANOIA BLUES (RD Davies)
This featured horns from the Mike Cotton Sound, a British jazz band, whose contributions led to them recording and playing live with The Kinks whenever commitments permitted. The dark lyrical content in which the speaker complained that he "can't trust nobody" and that he's "… lost on the river of no return" was offset by a light musical touch, but it, nevertheless, strikingly evoked paranoia and isolation.

HOLIDAY (RD Davies)
Following on from the previous track, Holiday painted a picture of escape from the stress of urban existence, although, even here, there was a dark side – the sea was polluted and the sun refused to shine, but our hero was determined to enjoy his time away.

SKIN & BONE (RD Davies)
From a time when the obsession with physical perfection was far less prevalent than it is today, here was an early warning about the perils of dieting and giving in to the pressures put on people to be unnaturally slim. Ray's slightly quavering delivery almost took this into T. Rex boogie territory.

ALCOHOL (RD Davies)
One of Ray's finest story songs, a stunningly economic lyric told how the pressures of modern life could lead a man to take refuge in alcohol and how it destroyed his life. Another fine contribution from the Mike Cotton Sound.

COMPLICATED LIFE (RD Davies)
Another song about the stress of modern life, concentrating on how it takes its toll on health and well-being, and how people increasingly feel the need to escape from the pressure. The musical arrangement brilliantly conjured up the weary, jaded feeling the lyrics described.

HERE COME THE PEOPLE IN GREY (RD Davies)

Taking its theme from the original inspiration for the album, this looked at the determination of one man, told that he was to be re-housed, to stand his ground against the powers that be. By the end of the song, he had begun to realise that he couldn't win, and a sense of resignation emerged.

HAVE A CUPPA TEA (RD Davies)

A curious hybrid of country-rock, hoedown and pub knees-up, this was a fun song based on Ray's gran's belief in the restorative powers of tea.

HOLLOWAY JAIL (RD Davies)

Influenced in equal measure by Delta blues and New Orleans jazz, Holloway Jail told the story of an upwardly mobile woman who fell in love with a conman and who now languished in prison after taking the blame for his deception. The lyric appeared to have been influenced by a family friend or an event from Ray's childhood.

OKLAHOMA USA (RD Davies)

Exploring a theme revisited on Celluloid Heroes and again on the Soap Opera album, this track looked at how people escape from their workaday world through the movies, dreaming of living the lives they see on screen.

A simple, wistful song, whose sparse musical arrangement featured just piano, guitar, and accordion.

UNCLE SON (RD Davies)

Fiercely political, this was an angry lyric, set to a slow blues, about the common man and how his life remained untouched by political aspirations. Along the way, it took sideswipes at unions, religion, and the military, all prepared to exploit people for their own ends.

MUSWELL HILLBILLY (RD Davies)

At Ray's insistence, working from the premise that Muswell Hillbillies should be seen as a cohesive whole, no singles were lifted from it in the UK. This would have been an ideal candidate and was a fine conclusion to a remarkably consistent collection.

CHAPTER 12 – EVERYBODY'S IN SHOWBIZ, EVERYBODY'S A STAR

If Muswell Hillbillies had not sold as well as RCA was expecting, it was still a critics' favourite, and The Kinks were still a strong live draw, especially in America. The hard work was paying off. The country that had shunned them for so long was now fanatical about them. Audiences were hooked onto every word and every move that Ray Davies made. The unlikely frontman, now the charismatic showman, was in command.

The rest of the band's members were living their own booze-fuelled lives, drifting away from their frontman. Dave, less extroverted than in his youth, would wallow in drinking with the crew on the road and with piano player John Gosling. They were making as much headway as they could in the States, five years too late.Now older and with real lives, they could not commit the time necessary for the three-month tours needed for making headway in the huge country. This would slow down their ascent on the American charts. Ray was now very much the focal point of the band. He was running the show. Brother Dave was being pushed more and more into the shadows. The two brothers' relationship had always been volatile, and the new situation was further aggravating it. Brothers are always at war, and always love each other. The Davies brothers took this a bit further than anyone else, and being creative and sensitive and on the road all the time didn't really help matters.

Warming up for the new album, they released 'Supersonic Rocket Ship'. The mini-hit saw their last appearance on Top Of The Pops for a decade. Whether they were getting long in the tooth or not, nothing stopped them from getting up to some of the old hi-jinx, including Ray pouring a pint of beer over Slade. The appearance helped the single to become a minor hit.

Their 1972-released double album, Everybody's In Showbiz, Everybody's A Star, was obviously affected by their recent hard touring of the States. The concept this time was about touring itself and its pros and cons. The schizophrenic attitude to the tough life of being in a touring band pervaded the record. There were songs detailing the life they were leading, the weary round of motels and long drives, and the highs of the gigs. It also features more melancholy songs; wondering just why they were pushing themselves through such a tough life, in a series of campy vaudevillian songs soaked in alcohol.
It was a keen observation of pop-star life, as ever cynical and witty in its view of the world. The cornerstone track of the album was 'Celluloid Heroes', which was the wordiest song Ray had come up with to date, a mass of lyrics that attempted to expose the illusion of stardom, all the time asking himself why he does it.

Everybody's In Showbiz came with a live album, capturing The Kinks at a time when they were most in touch with their audience, with the new, extroverted Ray in command of his faithful. Contrasted with their previous live album, Live At Kelvin Hall, an historic electric set with screaming girls from five years before, this was a more mature audience loving a band that had become like a secret society, a cult band.

In America they had a different audience, a post-'Lola' crowd that loved their good-time show. Ray's charismatic cheer-leading had made a real connection. The Kinks, that most bizarre of groups, were about to have a bizarre career change. Few groups in rock 'n' roll wait this long to break a market, and just when the band seemed to be reaching its use-by date they were fast-tracking it in America.

Whilst punk was a vindication of The Kinks, as several of the new breed celebrated their genius, The Kinks were not around to check it. The Jam put 'David Watts' back on the charts. Chrissie Hynde and her Pretenders put 'Stop Your Sobbing' into the top 20.

The Kinks were now hip, a curious place for them after all the years of neglect. Meanwhile, the canonisation of the group went into hyperdrive in the States, with Van Halen getting a huge hit with their inferior version of 'You Really Got Me', which managed to drain all the youthful effervescence and energy out of the original and replace it with heavy riffing and virtuosity.

The Kinks, now stripped of the theatricals, were moving closer and closer to hard rock themselves. If Schoolboys In Disgrace was a return to their rockier roots, they now moved further down this road, knocking all the clever edges off their sound and going resolutely blue-collar rock 'n' roll. This was a turnaround that suited their most junior member, Dave, who was still only 30. The band's guitar hero was waking up again after years of melancholy and being ignored by his older brother. In March 1977 they released Sleepwalker, which underlined Ray's return to rock 'n' roll, much to the relief of the band. The concepts were gone and the Kinks retuned to their hard-rock roots. Described by the American

press as "a phoenix rising from the ashes", the album was The Kinks gone American. Songs celebrated the pizzazz and speed of New York, a city that was buzzing 24 hours a day, like new resident, Ray Davies, himself. Sleepwalker, which was pitched directly at America, was nominally a hit there, selling 300,000 copies – 10 times the amount that Village Green Preservation Society had done – and going to number 21 in the charts. It was their biggest success for a decade. The 'Sleepwalker' single also got into the top 50. The Kinks were back, and even if they had lost a bit of what had made them fascinating in the first place, they still managed to retain enough eccentricity lurking just below the standard rock surface to make them remain interesting.

The songs on this album were:

LIFE ON THE ROAD (RD Davies)
A London A-Z song in Showbiz style to open the album in up-tempo-style, guiding the listener from Abbey Road to Praed St. and Pimlico. "Though there are bits of me in it, I wrote it for another character."

MR. BIG MAN (RD Davies)
A laid-back attack on the many music-biz moguls who'd ripped Ray off over the years.

SLEEPWALKER (RD Davies)
Built around a great Dave guitar riff as in the classic days of old, this story song told of "a vampire … somebody who feeds off people's lives rather than their blood."

BROTHER (RD Davies)
A provocative ballad, as the relationship between the two Davies brothers was not at its best around this time.

JUKE BOX MUSIC (RD Davies)
Another riff-driven rocker about a female Kinks fan living in the past with her Juke Box Music.

SLEEPLESS NIGHT (RD Davies)
Though written by Ray, Dave handled the lead vocals on the album's second somnambulistic song that faded out all too soon.

STORMY SKY (RD Davies)
A magnificently melodic piano-based song that was one of the album's highlights, transcending its clichéd meteorological allusions.

FULL MOON (RD Davies)
Ray walking in his sleep yet again, losing his identity and wondering just when he became the lunatic.

LIFE GOES ON (RD Davies)
The album concluded on a philosophical note – "Right or wrong, life will still go on."

Meanwhile, punk rock was raging in England, and the new generation's positive noises about The Kinks was reciprocated by The Kinks themselves. Whilst supporting the new bands, Dave acknowledged punk's similarities with The Kinks' early work. Dave was still hip enough to pick up on the energy of punk rock; after all, he was only five years older than some of the key players on the new scene. Success in America comes at a price, and now that The Kinks were on the fast track, the touring was becoming increasingly intense. John Dalton left them, explaining that their touring commitments had become too much, and he wanted to spend more time with his family. They replaced him with Andy Pyle, but when the band was working on the new album, Misfits, both Pyle and Gosling left as well.

The first single from Misfits, 'A Rock n Roll Fantasy', sang about the contradictions inherent in the rock 'n' roll world and the whole phoney circus. It was the band's first top-30 hit in America since 'Lola' seven years before. Misfits was not as successful as Sleepwalker, but it still consolidated their newfound success in America. It was again in a hard-rock vein, and the songs were built around a loose thread involving being the outsider – the misfit. The Kinks themselves, despite all their hard-won success, still felt outside the rock 'n' roll circus.

The songs on this album were:

MISFITS (RD Davies)
A lyric biographer, Johnny Rogan, called this "one of Ray's best for ages". It was combined with a Spanish guitar accompaniment to great effect. Considered by its writer as the track that tied the album together.

HAY FEVER (RD Davies)
The weakest song on the album was built around a litany of pollen counts, allergies, and sinus pains. Recorded in many keys and with many bass players, but with little result.

LIVE LIFE (RD Davies)
A single which earned the scorn of one Johnny Rotten: "What can you say about patronising, prattish, ill-conceived, calculated token gestures of 'understanding the scene, maaan' like this?" he told New Musical Express.

ROCK 'N' ROLL FANTASY (RD Davies)
Elvis Presley's death was announced while this song was being written in Ray's Manhattan apartment, a stark reminder to Ray and his fellow rock 'n' roll stars of their own mortality.

It was a time of reminiscing and looking backwards, which was perhaps understandable as the future looked bleak. The Kinks played live for the last time in 1996. There has been constant talk of a reunion, but the two brothers showed little interest in playing together again. Ray didn't even show for his brother's fiftieth birthday celebrations. The old feelings still remain, however, and on a 1998 solo album called Storyteller, released to tie in with his X Ray book, Ray celebrated his fractious relationship with his younger sibling.

The last 10 years have seen Ray Davies cement his reputation as one of the elder statesman of British rock. His autobiography has helped confirm this reputation, and his solo tours in theatres, where he plays his hits and tells stories of his amazing career, are great shows. In the meantime, brother Dave has been out playing and furthering his own solo career, albeit at a lower level.

Both brothers have had their problems in the past few years, Ray got shot in the leg whilst chasing a mugger in New Orleans in 2005, and Dave had a heart attack in the lift of the BBC whilst promoting his concept solo album Bug. Fortunately, they both seem finally to be on the mend, and there is always hopeful talk of The Kinks getting back together for one final hurrah. They met in 2005 after being inducted into the UK Hall of Fame. It was the first time the original lineup had been in a room together for years. They went for a curry afterwards and discussed recording one final album. So far nothing has come to fruition but the idea is there.

It's tantalising to see what they could come up with. If there was any band that would be suited to creating great material in their older years it would be The Kinks. After all, even at their youthful peak, Ray

Davies was writing the kind of songs that only years of experience would normally allow. A final album by The Kinks would perfectly bookend one of the most idiosyncratic careers in rock 'n' roll, and if, for once, they managed to get it promoted properly they could even return with all guns blazing.

One of the most influential bands of all time, with a stack of great albums that seemed to slip under rock's radar, The Kinks were a creative powerhouse for nearly three decades. Ray Davies at his best has quite simply been one of the greatest songwriters of all time, an equal to the Beatles with a unique vision all his own. He created the uniquely English sound and has influenced generations of musicians after him. All this time his younger brother Dave has been there fighting, arguing, and playing extraordinary gifted lead guitar – just check some of those early solos; the solo of 'You really Got Me' is perhaps the greatest guitar solo of all time and was played by a wild-eyed 17-year-old kid. The pair of them worked perfectly in tandem.

The Kinks were one of the greatest bands this country has ever produced, and their whole career, warts and all, has been a fascinating battle between music-business expectations and the emotional frailty, demons and extraordinary imagination of its frontman and his fractious relationship with his younger brother.

Pure genius.

There will never be another band like them.

God save the Kinks.

THE END